WITHDRAWN

This book belongs to the
Library of
HUGO L. DREWLER

THE PLACE OF JESUS CHRIST
IN
MODERN CHRISTIANITY

BY THE SAME AUTHOR

THE INTERPRETATION OF RELIGION
An Introductory Study of Theological
Principles

THE PLACE OF JESUS CHRIST
IN
MODERN CHRISTIANITY

BY

JOHN BAILLIE
M.A. (Edin.), D.Litt. (Edin.)

PROFESSOR OF SYSTEMATIC THEOLOGY IN EMMANUEL COLLEGE,
UNIVERSITY OF TORONTO; AUTHOR OF "THE INTER-
PRETATION OF RELIGION" AND "THE ROOTS
OF RELIGION IN THE HUMAN SOUL"

Carl A. Rudisill Library
LENOIR RHYNE COLLEGE

NEW YORK
CHARLES SCRIBNER'S SONS
1929

232
B15p

28762

232
B15p

28762

COPYRIGHT, 1929, BY

CHARLES SCRIBNER'S SONS

Printed in the United States of America

April 1953

TO

F. J. B.

10th April, 1919—*10th April*, 1929.

PREFACE

My endeavour in these chapters is to restate our Christian conviction about our Lord Jesus Christ in a form which shall avoid the many perplexing difficulties inherent in the traditional presentation of it, while yet losing hold of none of the great insights into spiritual truth which lay embedded within that traditional presentation and were the real secret of its marvellously powerful appeal to the human heart. If I have thus succeeded in making the smallest contribution to the end

> "That mind and soul, according well,
> May make one music as before,
>
> But vaster,"

I am more than rewarded.

The first draft of these chapters was hurriedly put together in June 1927, when I was asked, at a month's notice, to deliver a course of five lectures to the Midsummer Conference for Ministers and Religious Workers at Union Theological Seminary, New York. Shortly afterwards President Coffin and the Faculty and Directors of the Seminary did me the honour to suggest that the course should again be delivered in the Seminary, this time to the regular student audience under the terms of the Ely Foundation. For this purpose I subjected what I had written to a very thorough revision and expansion, so that it was now of a length to occupy eight lecture periods. The eight lectures were delivered last month, and they are now published for the Seminary as required by the deed of foundation. In preparing my manuscript for the press I have redistributed the matter into nine chapters, but have otherwise made little attempt to remove the traces of the lecturing style.

Had I, in being appointed to lecture on this very honourable foundation, been left entirely free to select my own subject, my mind would naturally have turned to one of two or three more limited and special regions of enquiry into which it has of late been inclined to wander, rather than to a broad and much-occupied field like the present one, where I could not hope to contribute anything new but only to help towards the clarification of what is already very old. Whether this would have been for better or for worse I do not know.

I welcome this opportunity of offering my warmest thanks to my many good friends at Union Theological Seminary, and particularly to President and Mrs. Coffin, for the great kindness shown me during my visit. Hearty thanks are due also to my friend and colleague,

Professor Richard Davidson, who read my manuscript and made a number of useful suggestions; to my friends, Mrs. John Dow of Toronto and Professor J. Y. Campbell of Yale University, who have once again done me great service by reading the proofs and correcting many little slips of mind and pen; and to my brother, the Reverend D. M. Baillie of Cupar-Fife, Scotland, whose talks with me last summer during many country rambles have been of much help to me in rewriting the chapter on Atonement.

JOHN BAILLIE.

TORONTO, 11th May, 1929.

CONTENTS

THE PLACE OF JESUS CHRIST
IN
MODERN CHRISTIANITY

CHAPTER I

THE PRESENT PERPLEXITY REGARD-
ING CHRISTOLOGY

I

THERE is no part of traditional religious belief which gives rise to so much perplexity in the minds of the men of our time as does the part bearing on what has traditionally been called the 'Person and Work of Christ.' In most of our communities there is to be found a surprisingly large number of men and women who are prevented from a whole-hearted sympathy with the Christian teaching and a whole-hearted participation in the life of the Christian Church by the necessity of making some kind of reservation just at this point. The doctrine of God the Father causes them no difficulty. They feel their human need and they believe that it can only be met by divine love. They share the Christian ideals of character and service and the Christian hope for the future of the soul. Many of them are glad when we say unto them, Let us go into the house of the Lord. But the doctrines of the Trinity and the Incarnation and the Atonement have never been anything else to them than a stone of stumbling and a rock of offence.

This state of affairs might, if it were necessary, be illustrated from many different sources. Appeal might be made, for instance, to the great literary figures both of the present day and of the last fifty years; for there cannot be many of us who have not at some time or another been struck by the comparatively small proportion of our poets and novelists and historians and essayists who have seemed to take seriously the Christian dogmas of our Lord's divinity and of salvation through His blood. I remember myself how even in my schooldays it was a constant source of uneasiness to me that so many of my earliest intellectual heroes and spiritual mentors—Wordsworth and Goethe, Carlyle and Emerson and Matthew Arnold and the rest—passed over this part of our spirit's heritage in so ominous a silence. Once these things were at the centre of our literature (as also of our music and our pictorial art)—think of the *Divina Commedia* and *Paradise Lost;* but now what place have they in such a representative book as the Poet Laureate's *The Spirit of Man?* Again, we might appeal to such impressions as we have happened to form with regard to the attitudes assumed towards the traditional Christian teaching by the youth at our universities. Or, fetching a wider compass, we might remind ourselves of the recent questionnaires regarding religious belief which have been distributed among the people at large both in America and in Great Britain. For there is no doubt that in the wider circle, hardly less than in the narrower one, one of the most searching questions proved to be 'Do you believe in the divinity of Christ?'[1] Then we might, if we cared, go back to the careful investigations carried out under the auspices of the Young Men's Christian Association into the religion of the British and American armies during the Great War. We find Principal D. S. Cairns summing up the British evidence in the following very significant words:

"There is practically universal respect and even reverence for Jesus Christ. This is quite plainly seen whenever the men disclose their real thoughts about Him. . . . He is recognized by all the serious thinking men as the best of the race. . . . But the whole deeper side of the Church's teaching about Jesus Christ seems to have little or no hold upon them except of the loosest

[1]In the summer of 1926 *The Nation and Athenæum* and *The Daily News* distributed among their readers a questionnaire in which the fifth question read as follows: 'Do you believe that Jesus Christ was divine in a sense in which all living men could not be said to be divine?' Of *The Nation's* readers who returned the questionnaire 35.7 per cent answered 'Yes,' and 61.4 per cent answered 'No.' Of the readers of *The Daily News* 68.9 per cent answered 'Yes,' and 28.89 per cent answered 'No.' The different results obtained from the readers of the 'highbrow' and the popular publications have their own significance. Mr. R. B. Braithwaite in his *State of Religious Belief* (London, 1927) sums up the whole evidence by saying that "only some 60 per cent" of Christians to-day "believe that Jesus Christ was divine in a quite modest sense of divine" (p. 62).

kind. Of Jesus as the Son of God, and as the Atoning
Sacrifice for the world, they have little or no knowledge at all. . . ."[1]

Finally, reference might be made to the great
difficulty experienced by Christian missionaries
working among peoples of high intellectual
standing, such as the Hindus or the educated
classes in China or Japan, in obtaining acceptance for the full traditional view of the Person of Christ. Those of us who recently read
that notable book *The Christ of the Indian
Road* could not fail to be impressed by two
things—how much the author had to tell us
about India's new willingness to acknowledge
the supremacy of Jesus' way of life, and how
little he had to tell us about any readiness on her
part to accept the catholic teaching about His
Person.

I believe, however, that were I to spend time
in illustrating the modern perplexity regarding
Christological belief from any or all of these
sources, I should be performing a largely
superfluous task, because most of us know quite
enough about that perplexity through our own
personal participation in it. For myself, I shall
frankly avow that if any division is to be made
between those who have always had trouble in
assimilating to their own thinking the traditional formulæ regarding the Person and Work

[1] *The Army and Religion*, p. 33.

of Christ and those who have had no such trouble, I am to be classed in the former group.

Where then does our difficulty lie?

The difficulty is not one but many; yet it does seem possible to point to one very general feeling of misgiving with which the orthodox Christological formulation constantly inspires us nowadays, and which seems to lie at the root of much of our perplexity regarding it. What we cannot help feeling is that, at least in the forms in which it has often been presented to us, it contains an element of something very like *mythology*.

Many of you must be familiar with Mr. Santayana's often-quoted chapter called "The Christian Epic" in his book on *Reason in Religion*. It is a very striking attempt to tell the Christian tale in what might be described as its crudest and least reflective form. Let me now try to retell this tale for you, with only this difference—that while Mr. Santayana dwells at length upon the story of creation, I shall dwell at greater length upon the story of redemption.

II

From the beginning there has reigned in the heavens, surrounded by a host of winged messengers called angels, an infinitely wise and righteous and kingly Being whose name is God. In the year 4004 B. C. He decided to create

this planet, and also to create as its chief in-
habitants a race of beings called man, who were
to be in some sort copies of Himself. The first
man and woman, called Adam and Eve, He
placed in a park in Mesopotamia, and told them
they might roam through it as they pleased, so
long as they did not attempt to eat the fruit of
one particular tree. Unfortunately, however,
they were soon incited to do this very thing by
one of God's own winged ministers, called
Satan, who had been cast out of the celestial
kingdom and was now ruler of a fiery under-
world of his own, called Hell. Adam and Eve
were created immortal, but the punishment of
their disobedience was death: in the first place
the decay and death of the body after a short
term of years on earth, and in the second place
the death of the soul which, instead of being
elevated to the celestial region where it might
company with God and His angels, would be
claimed by Satan and be condemned to burn
with him in the fires of Hell for ever. Moreover, not only did this punishment fall on
Adam and Eve who committed the sin, but also
on all their offspring, which is to say, on the
whole human race; each man and woman born
into the world now possessing congenitally that
unruly and corrupt nature which their first par-
ents had merely acquired, and also participating
in the guilt of their ancestors' transgression.

The dreadful result was that the whole race

of man, which God had created to company with Himself and be as His own beloved family, was now condemned, and that to the last man, to spend eternity not only in complete estrangement from Him but in physical and mental torture too awful to be imagined or described. Man himself could do nothing to mend matters, for not only was his own nature now thoroughly corrupted, but he was already implicated in Adam's transgression. As regards a large proportion, perhaps the majority, of the human race God was willing to let this state of things remain: these, says the Westminster *Confession of Faith*, "God was pleased, according to the unsearchable counsel of his own will, whereby he extendeth or withholdeth mercy as he pleaseth, for the glory of his sovereign power over his creatures, to pass by, and to ordain them to dishonour and wrath for their sin, to the praise of his glorious justice."[1] But with a certain select number of men and women God, in His love and pity and in order to manifest His own greater glory, was anxious to deal differently, and to find some means whereby He might, without in any way setting aside the proper demands of justice, rescue them from Satan and his Hell and restore them to fellowship with Himself in His Heaven. The selection was made, not according to any merit or desert on the part of those selected (for in that

[1] III, 7.

regard all are in like case), but according to
God's "mere good pleasure."[1]

But what plan of rescue was after all con-
ceivable? All men were bound by the laws of
justice to suffer the pains of Hell during infinite time, and God could not infringe the laws
of justice without compromising His glory and
acting contrary to His own just nature. There
was no way in which He could call upon man to
help, for nothing man could do, however meri-
torious, could avail to wipe out the record
against him. Was there then anything which
God might do? The difficulty here was that if
man had his punishment remitted in view of
some reparation which had been made by *God*,
the laws of justice would again be contravened,
because after all it was man who had incurred
the guilt. There was, however, one other possibility. God had a Son, who was of one essence with Himself and yet a different 'person'; this Son being indeed one of three 'persons'—Father, Son and Holy Ghost—united
in the one essential Deity. And now, out of
His infinite pity for mankind and His infinite
tenderness towards those whom He had selected for rescue, He proposed that this Son should
empty Himself of His celestial glory, and be
born on earth as the offspring of a Jewish
peasant maiden, and suffer death, and descend
into Hell for three days, before finally ris-

[1]Westminster *Shorter Catechism*, Q. 20.

ing from the dead and going back to Heaven to His Father. The death of One who was thus *both* God *and* man was the only thinkable means whereby man's rescue could be accomplished; for, in the celebrated words of St. Anselm,

"God will not do it because He ought not, and man will not do it because he cannot: therefore in order that God-and-man may do this, it is necessary that he who is to make this satisfaction should in his same person be perfect God and perfect man; for he cannot do it unless he be very God, nor ought unless he be very man."[1]

To this humiliation for the sake of the elect among mankind the Son consented in obedience and love. And in the year one of our era He was actually born in Bethlehem in Palestine, being known in the flesh as Jesus the son of Mary. He allowed Himself to fall into the hands of His enemies, and was hanged by them on the Cross, and then descended into Hell, and after three days rose again and ascended into Heaven, where He now sits at the right hand of God the Father. So the plan of rescue was completed, and now there is given to each of the elect "the grace of faith," whereby he is "enabled to believe" in its sufficiency and to accept it and apply it to his own case.[2] Moreover, this grace of faith is effective not only to the appropriation by the individual of the salvation thus of-

[1] *Cur Deus Homo*, Bk. II, Ch. VII.
[2] Westminster *Confession of Faith*, XIV, 1, 2.

fered, but also to the moral regeneration of all who receive it, so that the elect are gradually made more perfect in holiness. And when they die, instead of being cast into Hell with the rest of mankind, they are at once received into the celestial society. "The souls of the righteous," says the Westminster *Confession*, "being then made perfect in holiness, are received into the highest heavens, where they behold the face of God in light and glory, waiting for the redemption of their bodies; and the souls of the wicked are cast into Hell, where they remain in torments and utter darkness. . . ."[1]

Finally, at some future date which is known to no man, nor to the angels, nor even to the Son, but only to the Father, the Son will descend through the clouds to hold a last tribunal. All the dead will then be reunited to their old bodies. The Son will divide the elect from the non-elect and pass judgment on all. The latter will return to Hell, to live there in torment for ever, while the former, their bodies being now "made conformable to his own glorious body,"[2] shall be led by the Son into everlasting life with God in Heaven.

III

We shall all, I think, recognize that as at least one way in which the Christian tale has been told in every age. That account of it

---

[1] *Ibid.*, XXXII, 1.   [2] *Ibid.*, XXXII, 3.

would, I believe, have been generally recognized and approved by Athanasius, Augustine, Bernard, Thomas Aquinas, Luther, Calvin and all the Puritans, though there are certain details which one and another of these would have stated a little differently. This does not mean that the thought of these great men did not go beyond this recital—that was far indeed from being the case. But it does mean that they would not have repudiated this as a summary account of the general framework within which most of their thinking in this region was carried on, or at least as the starting-point from which it set out.

Yet to a large number of men and women of our day this great drama reads, not like a history, nor yet like a philosophy, but, as I have said, like a chapter from the world's mythology. The idea of a God who is three-in-one they cannot take seriously. They put the conception of the God-man on the same level as the centaurs. The notion of escape from eternal torment through the substitutionary value of the death of Jesus of Nazareth does not seem to touch the reality of their life and thought at any single point. And you and I understand these feelings of theirs well enough, and even share them ourselves in no small measure. The fault, we feel, is at least not all on one side. We cannot think that all this modern estrangement from the traditional epic of salvation is *wholly* due to spiritual obtuseness and corruption of heart on the part of our eagerly-seeking contemporaries. We are ready to acknowledge that in part at least it is due to some serious defect in the epic itself.

IV

Shall we then allow this Christian epic to pass, with the stories of Olympus and Valhalla, into the dim repertory of the past? Shall we, while continuing to worship One God and to cherish the hope of the divine destiny of the soul, while continuing also to admire the human figure of Jesus and profit by much that He taught, yet relegate the God-man and His Saving Deed to that same semi-lethal chamber of our minds in which Theseus and Siegfried now quietly sleep?

The question will, I believe, serve only to make us feel that there is another side, a tremendous other side, to this whole matter.

For, however difficult it may be to escape the impression that this Christian epic is in its essence but a splendid myth, yet I am myself convinced, and I think *most* of us are in the bottom of our hearts convinced, that somehow it reflects and embodies the most profoundly important truth that has ever presented itself to the mind of man. "And in Jesus Christ His only Son our Lord; who was conceived by the Holy Ghost; born of the Virgin Mary; suffered under Pontius Pilate; was crucified, dead and buried; He descended into hell; the third day He rose again from the dead; He ascended into heaven; and sitteth on the right hand of God the Father Almighty; from thence He shall come to judge the quick and the dead"—yes, in that recital there is contained, or at least behind the framing of it there lies, the most revealing ray of insight into the nature of reality and the meaning of human life that has yet lightened our mortal darkness. Nothing else, so much as this, has been "the light of men." The desire to have done with all mythology and to discard it in favour of a profounder type of knowledge called philosophy or science comes to us, of course, entirely from the Greeks. No people that has not been influenced by the Greeks has ever called a myth a myth or clearly made the distinction between a myth and something else that was better. Yet we here assert that behind this apparently mythical tale of God's Son coming to earth in human form and dying for our sins on a gallows-tree there is a realisation of truth that is in line with the very deepest divinings of Greek philosophy—as found especially in Socrates, Plato, Aristotle, Zeno and Plotinus; that is in line with them *and goes yet deeper*. I have myself drunk long and deeply at the fountain of this Greek wisdom, and I have companied also with the philosophers of later days more than most of you would think was quite good for me; yet I have come more and more to feel that this evangelic tale which the simple folk of the Western world have now been hearing during some fifty generations has that in it of deep discovery into the core of things which no philosophy has ever quite succeeded in filtering out for its own use.

Let us read something we all know by heart, and then let us ask ourselves a question about it:

> Rock of Ages, cleft for me,
> Let me hide myself in Thee;
> Let the water and the blood,
> From Thy riven side which flowed,
> Be of sin the double cure,
> Cleanse me from its guilt and power.
>
> Not the labours of my hands
> Can fulfil Thy law's demands;
> Could my zeal no respite know,
> Could my tears for ever flow,
> All for sin could not atone;
> Thou must save, and Thou alone.
>
> Nothing in my hand I bring,
> Simply to Thy cross I cling;
> Naked, come to Thee for dress,
> Helpless, look to Thee for grace;
> Foul, I to the fountain fly;
> Wash me, Saviour, or I die.
>
> While I draw this fleeting breath,
> When my eyelids close in death,
> When I soar to worlds unknown,

See Thee on Thy judgement throne,
Rock of Ages, cleft for me,
Let me hide myself in Thee.

Now what kind of feeling has been upper-most in our minds as we read these familiar couplets? Did we whisper to ourselves, "After all, how grotesque it is!"? Or did we whisper rather, "After all, how profoundly *right* it is, and how satisfying to the soul!"? Did the read-ing awake a memory of something past and done with, or did it rather cause the deepest chords in our spiritual beings to sound their overtones in tune? We shall no doubt answer very variously, but I think that for most of us the only quite true answer would be that, in proportions however individual, we felt some-thing of *both* these responses. We might have selected, instead of "Rock of Ages," that fine hymn of Newman's with the climax:

O generous love! that He, who smote
In Man for man the foe,
The double agony in Man
For man should undergo.

Or we might have taken Cowper's hymn, equally noble in its poetic impulse:

There is a fountain filled with blood
Drawn from Emmanuel's veins;
And sinners, plunged beneath that flood,
Lose all their guilty stains.

And no doubt, if we had taken either of these, there would be some variation in the relative strength and readiness of the two responses. But for almost every one of us both responses would still be there in some quite sensible degree.

For myself, though vividly experiencing in my own mind and heart both these responses to all such presentations of the evangelic tale, I have no doubt at all as to which of the two is the more significant and springs from the deeper root in my spirit's life. We of the nineteenth and twentieth centuries have, by the grace of God, been privileged to witness a more remarkable advance in scientific, theoretic knowledge than has fallen to the lot of any age since the great age of Greece. We are all of us grateful sharers in this new spiritual wealth, eager to avail ourselves of its opportunity to the fullest possible extent, and unwilling to allow any part of our inherited mental furniture to escape its frankest criticism. But we must not exaggerate the real extent of our new store or misunderstand its nature. No mistake could be cruder, no 'Idol of the Theatre' could be more childish, than the assumption that because we know more than our fathers did about the movements of the stars or the inside of the atom or the origin of specific differences in living organisms, or still more that because we have harnessed to our use the forces of electricity and radioactivity and have built ourselves the telephone and the radio and the aeroplane, we have therefore any greater insight into the ultimate meaning of life and the ultimate nature of the Most High God. For it does not take much burrowing in the buried riches of the past, nor yet does it take a very penetrating awareness of our own souls' needs, to make us realise that in the deepest things of the spirit men like Socrates and Marcus Aurelius and St. Paul and St. Augustine had at least as true a judgement and as keen a vision as any of us moderns is likely to attain. When the question is, "What are the laws of the electrical constitution of matter?" or, "How am I to build an internal-combustion engine?" then indeed we moderns have it over all our forefathers. But when the question is, "What must I do to be saved?" or, "What is the ultimate purport of existence?" then you and I feel that we can often sit at the feet of those ancients in an almost silent humility. How much, when at last the long light of history falls upon these "foremost files of time" in which we are now living, will it be decreed that we have really added to the soul's interior treasure? Perhaps much less than the pride of any of us would now allow us to believe. But at all events let it not be written of us that we have despised our common heritage as "the heirs of all the ages." The wise remark has recently been made that "the wastefulness of re-

action against the past is a grave impediment to
the progress of man."[1]

Consequently, however keenly aware we may
be of the distance we have travelled since the
days when the evangelic tale was first put together in the traditional form in which I have
here set it down, we must be even more careful to give full weight to that other feeling we
have—that in this tale lies hidden the purest
gold of divine truth which is yet in the possession
of the human soul. It was this tale which, nearly
two thousand years ago, brought to the Mediterranean world the greatest liberation of spirit
that the history of the race has ever known, con-
quering alike the glory that was Greece and
the grandeur that was Rome, and finally bringing the whole living riches both of classic art
and of classic philosophy to the feet of the Galilean. It is this tale which has made our Eu-
rope and our West, softening the proud hearts
of all our Northern races. Yet more important
than any of these historical reflections is our
own sure perception that somehow in this gospel of "God sending his own Son in the likeness of sinful flesh, and for sin, to condemn
sin in the flesh," we are touching, as far as has
yet been given us, very rock-bottom of spiritual
reality and finding there just the one thing that
is fully adequate to our spirit's need.

[1] *Times Literary Supplement*, London, 12th May, 1927, p. 329.

Indeed there is more to be said even than that. For there is undeniably a certain sense in which the Christian message, far from having fallen into disrepute, is experiencing in this very age of ours something that amounts to a genuine renaissance of its life. However sorely puzzled our day and generation may find itself over the Catholic Christology taken as a whole, yet I believe that it is making such a rediscovery of *the spirit of the man Jesus* as has hardly been made in all the Christian ages. It seems to me that with every year that passes the hold of the spirit of Christ upon our current ideals is becoming more securely established. Think of the grip that the Man of Nazareth is at last beginning to have on our thinking concerning international relations! Think again how at last our consciences are beginning to awaken to the social implications of His teaching, so that we are coming to suspect that He really meant what He said about giving meat to the hungry and drink to the thirsty and healing our sick and ministering to those who are in our prisons! Thus we have begun to make rediscovery of the power which He believed to be in love; but think also of how we have begun to wonder whether He was not right about the power that lies in *faith!* Think of the new weight of meaning that modern psychology has found in sayings like "All things are possible to him that believeth" and "Thy faith

hath made thee whole"! The fact is that no student of our contemporary general literature can
be unaware of the change which has come over
the tone of it in the last twenty years, and even
in the few years that have gone by since the
War, with reference to the spirit of Christ. And
I might refer once again to the witness of such
a book as *The Christ of the Indian Road*. "As
the physical atmosphere," we read, "becomes
heavy with moisture, so heavy that it is precipitated into rain, so the spiritual atmosphere
of India is becoming heavy with interest in
Jesus Christ and is on the verge of and is actually being precipitated into Christian forms and
Christian expression."[1] "The cross," we read
again, "has become intelligible and vital. Up to
a few years ago one was preaching against a
stone wall in preaching the cross in India."[2]
But now Mahatma Gandhi has "put the cross
into politics."[3] And the author ventures on this
generalisation: "I believe that the lips of the
world are dumb and silent before the question
of finding anything better. In the realm of
character Jesus has the field."[4] This rediscovery of Christ may indeed be a very partial one,
and very far from carrying us all the way towards a rehabilitation of the Christian evangel,
but at least it presents a happy other side to our
Christological perplexities. One of our leading

[1]*Op. cit.*, pp. 83 f.   [2]*Ibid.*, p. 91.
[3]*Ibid.*, p. 88.   [4]*Ibid.*, p. 51.

theologians recently concluded a most competent presentation of the Christian faith by dis-
consolately remarking that at present that faith
lay under a cloud of disbelief, but that it had
been under such clouds before and had emerged,
and might be expected to emerge again. But I
felt that he had only one eye open to what is
happening in our time.

And now the question is how, if we keep both
eyes open to this matter, we can bring them into
clear focus with one another. The present situation is eminently unsatisfactory. Our generation
is more perplexed than any other generation has
ever been over the gospel tale of our Lord's Person and Work, yet, first, we are deeply conscious
that somehow in this tale is enclosed the only
balm for our soul's woe, and, second, the spirit
of our Lord's life, and of His cross, have laid
hold on us in a way that is strangely new. What
are we to do?

CHAPTER II

ALTERNATIVE LINES OF SOLUTION

I

DURING the years 1818 to 1831 there lectured in neighbouring classrooms in the University of Berlin two very great thinkers who regarded one another's methods of handling the religious problem with deep distrust. Looking back at the controversy across the hundred intervening years, we can now see that they did not stand quite so far apart from each other as they themselves supposed, being both alike children of the same Romantic age. Nevertheless they did stand for two significantly different attitudes towards our modern Christological perplexity, and the difference between them still represents the main alternative with which we are faced in trying to find a way out of this perplexity. The one thinker was Hegel, the other was Schleiermacher.

II

Let us look first at the line of solution followed by Hegel. Its general principle may be very simply stated. What it recommends us to

do is to accept quite frankly the mythological
character of the Christian tale and surrender
altogether its claim to be directly or literally
true, yet to continue to regard it as appropriately
and beautifully *symbolising* the deepest philosophic truth. Those who adopt this solution
would leave the old Christology quite untouched
in its detail, but would apply to the whole some
such qualifying epithet as 'mythological' or
'symbolical' or 'allegorical' or (to mention an
adjective often used by Hegel himself) 'pictorial.' Hegel's way of putting the matter is that
religion never gives us truth save in the form of
a *Vorstellung* or image, it being only philosophy
that can lead us to that exacter kind of knowledge which is alone adequate to its object, and
which he calls the *Begriff* or concept. In general philosophy Hegel was a champion of the
kind of outlook known as absolutism, and it is
true that such an attitude to religion has often
been closely associated with absolutism in philosophy. As early as the middle of the seven-
teenth century we find it clearly represented by
Spinoza, who wrote a treatise to show that the
conflict between faith and philosophy could be
overcome only by recognising "that faith does
not so much demand that its doctrines should be
true, as that they should be *pious, i. e.*, suited to
incline our hearts to moral obedience"; [1] while
among contemporary thinkers we find it repre-

[1] *Tractatus Theologico-Politicus*, Ch. XIV.

sented in its very baldest form by that learned Italian, Benedetto Croce, who tells us outright that "religion is identical with myth."[1] However, the attitude is one which seems to combine readily enough with a variety of other philosophical outlooks. You will find it in the works of several of the philosophers of Roman Catholic modernism, such as Blondel and Le Roy. And you will find it in Mr. Santayana, to whose presentation of the 'Christian Epic' I referred in the last chapter. Yet Mr. Santayana differs from Hegel in that, being on the whole more of a Comtian positivist than an absolutist, he looks upon Christian dogma as being allegorical, not of a metaphysical or cosmical, but of a purely moral meaning. The strength of the Christian system, he tells us, lay in the fact that

"all its parts had some significance and poetic truth, although they contained or needed to contain, nothing empirically real. The system was a great poem which, besides being well constructed in itself, was allegorical of actual experience, and contained, as in a hieroglyph, a very deep knowledge of the world and of the human mind. For what was the object that unfolded itself before the Christian imagination, the vision that converted and regenerated the world? It was a picture of human destiny. It was an epic, containing, as it were, the moral autobiography of man."[2]

[1] *Logic as the Science of the Pure Concept*, E. tr., p. 444.
[2] *Interpretations of Poetry and Religion*, pp. 88 f.

sense should take a course in Plato (perhaps with the help of Prof. J. A. Stewart's book on *The Myths of Plato*), and should acquaint themselves with his profound teaching that, since philosophy deals only with truths that are timeless, and since history, though dealing with events in time, must necessarily fail us with regard both to sheer beginnings and to future events, we must at these points have recourse to telling a myth, which is just the Greek for a story. Furthermore, it is certain that none of our human thoughts of the Divine can ever be wholly adequate to their infinite object. What God is in Himself must ever remain unimaginable to finite minds, and ineffable to finite lips. We cannot hope that any thought or word of ours should hold His whole Being in its grasp; the highest task we can set ourselves is only to discover which aspects of our poor human experience afford us the least misleading clue to the transcendence of His glory. To forget this is not merely bad philosophy, it is bad religion; for true religion has always taught that His ways are not as our ways but are past finding out. Hence there is a true sense in which all our human thoughts of God may be said to have in them an element of unavoidable symbolism.

But after all there is a difference between this symbolic quality which must ever attach to our human thinking about ultimate reality and a

symbolism which is set down as such because it
fails to satisfy even our own deepest and most
philosophic reflection. And so, when it is proposed that we modern Christians should be willing to regard the whole Christological and so-
teriological scheme as being merely what we call
symbolic myth, there is no end to the objections
that rise up in our minds. For one thing, read
the story in as symbolic a sense as you list, yet
there will keep breaking through the veils of it
a true history—the history of One who lived in
the flesh in our world, and *an actual event*—His
death upon an Eastern hill. Indeed for us these
literal things break through the symbolism even
more irrepressibly than they did for our fore-
fathers, because we to-day have reached a deeper
appreciation of the historic Jesus than they ever
possessed. Secondly, can we believe that what is
known to be no more than a beautiful imaginative invention can ever have the power over
men's hearts and lives which the Christian gospel has had—making them face bereavement
and death with brave hearts and vanquishing
their animal natures, day by day, in open battle?
Is it not very certain that, if our faith ever did
come to be regarded in this subdued light, the
ordinary man would soon begin to look elsewhere for the fulfilment of his heart's desire?
There is deep understanding behind Mr. Bernard Shaw's dictum that "No dogma can be a

legend."[1] But finally, there is a third objection, perhaps the most significant of all. The fact is that the difficulty we have with the traditional Christology and soteriology would not really be met at all by the proposal to regard the whole scheme as a significant symbolism. Many of the perplexities to which it gives rise in our minds would remain the same, no matter whether we regarded it as myth or as metaphysic. The attitude of the Hegelians to Christian dogma has in one sense been notoriously uncritical. "The difficulty," as Canon Quick has wittily remarked, "is to discover anything which modernists of this school can conscientiously reject."[2] They have always seemed, as it were, to swallow the tradition *whole*, without bothering about any preliminary discrimination of the gristly parts from the good meat. Yet it has constantly been felt that in so doing they were paying the tradition a more

---

[1]With equal wisdom Mr. Shaw adds: "This does not mean that we should throw away legend and parable and drama: they are the natural vehicles of dogma; but woe to the churches and rulers who substitute the legend for the dogma, the parable for the history, the drama for the religion. Better by far declare the throne of God empty than set a liar and a fool on it. . . . But who has ever refused to accept a good legend with delight *as* a legend? The legends, the parables, the dramas, are among the choicest treasures of mankind. . . . Every one of these legends is the common heritage of the human race; and there is only one inexorable condition attached to their healthy enjoyment, which is that no one shall believe them literally" (*Back to Methuselah*, Preface, pp. lxxv-lxxvi).

[2]*Liberalism, Modernism and Tradition*, p. 48.

left-handed compliment than at first sight appeared, because it was after all so obvious that (if we may be allowed to carry the metaphor so far) they were willing to take it in the lump only because they never really swallowed it at all. Since it was all only symbolism, since they took none of it quite seriously and literally, it was not worth while to raise ecclesiastical dust by any serious attempt at a revision of its detail. But to those who feel on the one hand that in the Christian religion we are confronted with the most satisfying revelation of the nature of ultimate reality to which we can by any means attain, and on the other hand that the traditional presentation of it is at many points without meaning to the contemporary mind, this solution can never be sufficient.

III

It would seem then that we have no choice but to adopt the alternative line of solution which I have connected particularly with the name of Schleiermacher. It also may be very summarily described. It consists in taking the traditional Christology and soteriology as *intending* to give us direct truth, or at least truth of as direct a kind as is ever available to us, and then rethinking or recasting them in such a way as to make them adequate to our deepest and most recent insights. Instead of leaving them untouched and either relegating them to our museums or setting them as ritual ornaments upon our altars, we are to reshape them for active use as instruments of our most reflective thought. Such a reshaping will necessarily involve the frankest and most outspoken criticism, but this very criticism will in its way be an index of the value we set upon the thing criticised. To take an example, the Hegelians have always set the dogma of the Trinity at the very centre of their philosophy of religion. "The Trinity," writes the Scottish Hegelian, John Caird, "is the distinctively Christian idea of God."[1] But the same writer warns us that here as always faith "presents the spiritual to us through images borrowed from the sensible and the eternal, and it is only by rising above the symbolical or representative form that we can grasp the reality which they 'half reveal and half conceal.' "[2] Schleiermacher, on the other hand, gives no place at all in the body of his system to the doctrine of the Trinity, treating of it only in a brief appendix. We may or may not think he is right in this (and of that more below), yet we cannot but have something of the feeling that behind his silence there lies more real *belief*, and a deeper appreciation of Christian truth as a whole, than behind the Hegelians' ready speech.

Now we need not pretend that such a recon-

[1] *The Fundamental Ideas of Christianity*, Vol. I, p. 58
[2] *Ibid.*, p. 55.

struction of the traditional Christology as will
satisfactorily meet all our modern questions
about it is going to be either an easy or an entirely painless task. I may illustrate the nature
of the difficulty in the following way. Not long
ago I had the pleasure of listening to an after-
dinner speech by a very outstanding preacher of
our time, in which he inveighed most eloquently
and tellingly against the reduced and watery
form in which the Christian gospel is often presented to us nowadays. Where, he asked, are
those massive old conceptions of sin and damna-
tion, of salvation and the new birth, of atonement for sin and imputed righteousness, which
once stood at the centre of the evangelic appeal?
And what, in particular, has happened to the
Cross, which once was a shewing-forth of God's
love, but is now only an exhibition of human
heroism, worthy, not of our worship, but only
of our applause? My own fundamental sympathies, as I listened, were entirely with the
speaker, yet I felt that he showed an insufficient
patience with the difficulty of our contemporary
situation. I felt, indeed, that much of what he
said might be applied, not only to the Christian
tradition but, *mutatis mutandis*, to the religious
tradition of any race. There must, for example,
be many a Hindu who, when asked to set aside
his cruder Brahmanism in favour of our higher
Christian gospel, cries out to the missionary, "It
is easy for you to pick holes in our traditional

religion, but after all what profound spiritual insights lie embedded in these admittedly imperfect conceptions of *brahma* and *atman* and *maya* and *karma* and *bhakti!*" And profound spiritual insights *do* lie embedded in them, though it must be a task of immense difficulty to filter out these insights in such a way that they can be made use of without at the same time holding men down to those aspects of Brahmanism which Christianity has definitely transcended. Now it is true that the difficulty with which we of to-day are faced with regard to the old Christology is not only infinitely less in degree than this, but in part also of a different kind, our problem being not so much to disengage what is valuable in the old presentation from other things in it that are entirely without value, as rather to reinterpret and rearrange the whole in a way which will better bring out its true significance. But for all that the parallel has something in it. It is easy to tell men that they have not yet succeeded in taking up into their contemporary thinking all the values embedded in the traditional system, and it is very difficult indeed to tell them how this can be done.

Moreover there is another thing to be said. The matter is sometimes presented by the more nervous champions of orthodoxy as if we moderns, in desiring to reopen this whole issue of Christological formulation, were wantonly disturbing a magnificent edifice of ancient thought which, after many centuries of patient hammering and chiselling, had reached a finally triumphant completion at the Councils of Nicæa and Chalcedon. Yet the real truth is that this Christological question was always more or less of a difficulty for Christian thought, and that we are now doing no more than making a fresh attack upon a problem that was never really settled in a satisfactory way. The history of Christian theology during the first five centuries of its existence is, as a matter of fact, more than anything else a history of Christological perplexity. And if this perplexity seemed, with the coming of the Dark Ages, to give way to a contented Chalcedonian orthodoxy, that was not entirely because a satisfying solution had now at last been found, but partly because a kind of paralysis had begun to take possession of men's powers of independent thought. That is why, during our modern period, when the mind has been coming to its own again, the Christological problem has appeared to raise its head more insistently than ever. I have always felt that no good is done by assuming too reverential an attitude towards the progress of dogma in the early ages of the Church. The story does indeed read as a magnificent testimony to the compelling greatness and glory of Jesus Christ and the reality of the spiritual awakening which His gospel had brought to that whole Mediterranean world. Moreover, a renewed and more patient study of

the fundamental plot of it will usually be rewarded by the discovery that behind even its
most unreal debates there lay hidden, however
deep buried in the sawdust of the pedant's work-
shop, issues that are of real import for the understanding of the soul's life with God. And
we do, I think, almost invariably have the feeling that, as the lists were then drawn, the Church
Catholic was fighting on the better of the two
sides. Nevertheless it may be doubted whether
the story reads as one of the most successful
chapters in the history of the intellectual
achievement of our race. "If," says Mr. Ed-
wyn Bevan, "we are concerned to maintain that
with Christianity something new of unique value
entered the world, we must face fairly the aspect of deterioration which the Christian world
offers to the classical humanist. . . . We may
believe that Christianity had enriched life with a
new experience, and yet recognize that the minds
at work upon the matter of life had not the same
elasticity and liberty of movement as the minds
which in the fourth century B. C. had been
brought to play upon the experience, poorer in
this particular, of the ancient Athenian."[1] Some,
indeed, may feel inclined to press a further criticism. Here is what one recent writer says:

"Controversy was long drawn out and often conducted with great bitterness. The language which the

[1] *Hellenism and Christianity*, pp. 110-111.

combatants thought fit to use in speaking of their opponents suggests that in their zeal for what they believed to be correct theological doctrine about their Lord they had forgotten for a moment their Lord's precepts about the tempers He looked for in His followers. If the conclusions reached by the councils were infallible, they were reached by the help of those who were fallible enough in their loyalty to the spirit of Christ."[1]

One is reminded of a well-known remark of Voltaire's about the Jansenist controversies— that each party vied with the other for a hundred years as to which loved God most suitably and which could most effectively harass the other. But at all events it is true that, looked at from a purely intellectual point of view, the Christological controversies of the early centuries are not tremendously impressive to us. The modern student often finds it difficult to follow their tortuosities with that liveliness of interest with which the noblest chapters in the history of thought have been accustomed to inspire him.

Thus it is that in our own day the Christian consciousness is finding itself thrown back afresh upon its powers of independent reflection. It is to the task which thus presents itself that this little book will try to make a humble contribution. Our aim will be to set forth as clearly as we can what we believe to be true about Jesus Christ

[1] D. M. Ross, *The Christ of Faith and the Jesus of History*, p. 131.

and His relation to our religious life, availing ourselves eagerly of the hereditary forms of thought and expression wherever these seem likely to help us, but not hesitating to seek out new and different forms wherever our thinking demands them. It is plain that in doing this we must start from the very foundations. But the foundations of Christology are set deep in the essential experience of the Christian fellowship. And so we must begin our rethinking by making sure that we understand what that experience is.

CHAPTER III

THE CHRISTIAN FELLOWSHIP

I

THE Christian Church, regarded as an organised historical entity, had its rise nineteen hundred years ago in the frequent gathering together in a certain upstairs room in Jerusalem of a little band of strangers from the North. There was one meeting especially, which took place on the Jewish festival of Pentecost, and which seems to have impressed itself on their minds as marking the real beginning of things. At this time the band was so small that a single room could serve them, and so obscure that few in the city can have known of their existence. But in less than twenty years it was being said in far-away Macedonia that they (or their emissaries) had "turned the world upside down"; [1] and within less than three hundred years the whole Roman Empire and known world were found acknowledging the spiritual supremacy of the movement which had thus been set on foot.

What was there, then, about these little meet-

[1] *Acts* xvii, 6.

ings in the upstairs room that had in it the secret of such tremendous spiritual power, making them the starting-point of the greatest religious movement the world has ever seen? The only account we possess of what was done at these meetings is a very short and summary one, but for all that it contains the necessary clue. "They devoted themselves," we are told, "to the instruction given by the apostles [the original members of the group] and to *koinōnia*, breaking bread and praying together."[1] In ordinary usage this word *koinōnia* meant simply partnership or joint ownership, but it is clear that the little band were using it in a sense of their own and to denote something new that had come into their experience—and through their experience into the world; and we can only translate it as 'Christian fellowship.' With whom then was this fellowship enjoyed? The answer must be that it was at the same time a fellowship with one another and with the Spirit of God. As it has been excellently put, "the word in this specific sense would appear to denote a fellowship which was not merely a fellowship of believers *inter se*, nor yet a fellowship of the believers individually with the Spirit, but a complex experience which included both."[2] In other words, we have here to do with a relatively new relationship in which men found

[1] *Acts* ii, 42: *cf.* Moffatt's translation.
[2] C. Anderson Scott in *The Spirit* (ed. Streeter), pp. 137 f.

themselves standing both to one another and to God.

What was this new relationship? Here again I believe it is possible to answer the question by pointing to a single word which the early Christians adapted to their own use, and which soon came to be thought of as summing up in itself more of the true inwardness of the Christian fellowship than could be put into any other term. This word is *agapē*. Since it is all but unknown to us outside the Christian use of it,[1] it is a little difficult to know how to render it in another language. In English perhaps we can only call it 'love,' but the trouble with this word is that it covers also the Greek *erōs*, which the New Testament always most scrupulously avoids. When we speak in English of Christian 'love,' we are in danger of leaving behind us a certain suggestion of weak sentimentalism which is totally absent from the New Testament language. The makers of the Authorised Version were alive to this danger and fell back on the Latin word 'charity,' but unfortunately this word has now acquired a changed (shall we say a debased?) meaning in our language, and can no longer serve us here. It has always seemed to me that the really best way of rendering the

[1]A few doubtful instances of the occurrence of the word in pagan writings are mentioned in the new edition of Liddell and Scott's lexicon *in loc.*; also in the new edition of A. Deissmann's *Light from the Ancient East* (English translation, 1927, pp. 22 n. and 75–76 n.), and in the same writer's *Neue Bibelstudien*, pp. 26 f.

meaning of *agapē* is to translate it as 'fatherliness' when it applies to God and as 'brotherliness' when it applies to man; but the difficulty is that often it is used in such a way as to include both applications, and then we are reduced to saying simply 'love.' Indeed, as we saw, it is of the very nature of this *agapē* that it should cover both applications in one. From first to last it is regarded as a sort of triangular relationship in which (a) the Christian's attitude to God is very closely related to (b) his attitude to his Christian brethren, and in which his attitude to his Christian brethren is modelled after the pattern of (c) God's attitude to him. "They devoted themselves to fellowship, breaking bread and praying together"; and it is significant that this very practice of breaking bread together soon came to be spoken of simply as the *Agapē* or 'Love.'

The secret of the little band's influence, then, lay in the fact that in its meetings it was enjoying this *koinōnia* of *agapē*, this fellowship of Christian love. It must now be our business to understand how this fellowship worked out in the actual detail of life. Perhaps we can take a first step by instituting a certain comparison. In the age when Christianity was born, the finest souls in the world of Graeco-Roman culture were drawing their spiritual nourishment from the Stoic philosophy. At the centre of that philosophy there stood the noble conception of the

universe as *una civitas hominum divomque,* "one
great city of gods and men." Here we have one
of the most influential conceptions that have
ever been put before the human mind, and
Prof. Gilbert Murray has gone so far as to say
that "the greater number of our common religious metaphors are apparently derived from
it."[1] Now I know of no better way of summaris-
ing the New Testament teaching about the fellowship of Christian love than to say that it conceives the universe, not as one great city, but
rather as one great family in which one's self,
one's fellow men and God are all in different
ways included. It is in accordance with this inclusive conception that the accepted Christian
name for God becomes 'Father' and the accepted name for a fellow man becomes 'brother'; it having often been remarked that in the
New Testament these terms are not used in
their primary meaning of natural kinship, as de-
noting that God made us and that as children of
Adam we are all of one blood, but in the quite
different ethical and 'adoptive' sense that God
deals with us, and that we ought to deal with
our fellows, in the spirit of family affection.

II

But if we are to understand in any detail
what the Christian fellowship of love imports,
we must look separately at its two constituent

[1] *Essays and Addresses,* p. 183.

parts; though in doing so we must be careful
to remember that the fellowship is in its very
nature an organic and indivisible unity, the sum
of whose separate parts can never be quite equal
to the whole.

Let us look first at *agapē* as it obtains between man and man. Here, as we have seen,
the key word is 'brother,' and the literature of
the early centuries makes it very clear that
the associations of this word were as precious
to the Christians as its habitual use by them
appeared remarkable to their pagan neighbours. "They are angry with us," writes Tertullian, "because we call one another brethren."[1]
The earliest name for the human side of the
koinōnia was just "the brotherhood" (ἀδελφότης);[2] and the phrase "the whole brotherhood throughout the world" (πᾶσα ἡ ἐν κόσμῳ
ἀδελφότης)[3] appears as an early synonym for
the Church Catholic. "To understand how fixed
and frequent was the title," says Harnack, "to
understand how truly it answered to their life
and conduct, one has only to study, not merely
the New Testament writings, but Clemens
Romanus, the Didache, and the writings of the
apologists."[4]

[1] *Apol. adv. Gentes*, XXXIX.

[2] *Cf. I Peter* ii, 17; v, 9; etc.

[3] *Vide* von Harnack, *Mission and Expansion of Christianity*, E.
tr., Vol. II, pp. 14 ff., and T. M. Lindsay, *The Church and the
Ministry in the Early Centuries*, p. 21.

[4] *Op. cit.*, Vol. II, pp. 9 f.

The *locus classicus* for the anatomy of brotherly love is St. Paul's great "Hymn of *Agapē*" in the thirteenth chapter of First Corinthians. We need only remind ourselves of its central verses:

"Love is very patient, very kind. Love knows no jealousy; love makes no parade, gives itself no airs, is never rude, never selfish, never irritated, never resentful; love is never glad when others go wrong, love is gladdened by goodness, always slow to expose, always eager to believe the best, always hopeful, always patient."[1]

Keeping that and the whole literature in mind, one might venture to define Christian brotherly love as the transference, by an act of imaginative sympathy, to all those with whom we have in any wise to do, of those sentiments of tenderness and affection which even the meanest of us bestow upon our own flesh and blood.

Yet such a definition is far from containing all that needs to be said, because familiar words like 'tenderness' and 'affection' are no more sufficient than is the bare word 'love' itself to suggest the deepest elements in Christian *agapē*. I think what strikes one most about the Christian way of loving as it is set forth in the New Testament is this—that it is a love for the sake of the beloved, a love which seeks to benefit, not ourselves who love, but those on whom our

[1] *I Cor.* xiii, 4–7; Moffatt's translation.

love is poured, a love that seeks not to be min-
istered unto but to minister, or, as the late
Baron Friedrich von Hügel finely expressed it,
"a love which loves, not in acknowledgement of
an already present lovableness, but in order to
render lovable in the future what at present
repels love."[1] That is where *agapē* differs from
Eros. Its guiding principle is not a desire to give
ourselves pleasant company, but a desire to help
and save our brothers. So, in an evil world, it
comes to be above all else a *redemptive* love:
and perhaps redemptive or redeeming love is
after all the only fully adequate rendering of
agapē.

But now this redemptive character of Christian love and brotherliness carries with it another implication, and it is not until we realise
this implication that we penetrate to the heart of
the matter. For there is no conviction more
deeply embedded in New Testament thought
than that, if love is really to be redemptive, it
must be a *suffering* love—a love that involves
pain and renunciation and sacrifice and very
death itself. The world being what it is, and
sin being what it is, there can be no effective
helping or saving of our fellows except through
self-sacrifice. The principle of this vicarious
suffering may be seen in all family life and
even in the lesser kinships of the animal crea-

[1] *Essays and Addresses on the Philosophy of Religion, Second
Series*, p. 160.

tion, as when a mother gladly suffers pain for
the sake of her child's welfare or a mother-hen
braves many a danger for the protection of her
brood. But what is distinctive about the Christian fellowship is its realisation and utilisation of
this particular movement of natural instinct as
holding within it the main secret of the further
spiritual development of the race, and its consequent imaginative extension of it to all those
who in any way need our help. To bear one another's burdens, St. Paul tells the Galatians, is
to fulfil the underlying principle of the Christian fellowship. "It is the exercise of this noblest
sort of love," writes Tertullian at the beginning
of the third century, "that leads many to put a
brand on us. 'See,' they say, 'how these men love
one another . . . and how ready they are even
to die for one another.'"[1] This is the great spiritual discovery for which Christianity stands, and
it is certain that it was in the nature of a discovery
even to men who had been reared in the faith
of Israel. What the Jew had here to learn may,
from one point of view have been hardly more
than a subtle readjustment, a turn of the screw,
yet it is this turn of the screw that has made
our Christian civilisation. Comparing Jewish be-
nevolent righteousness (*chesed*) with Christian
agapē, that learned Jew of our time, Dr.
Claude Montefiore, allows that the latter stands
for "something more venturous, more self-sac-

[1] *Apol. adv. Gentes*, XXXIX.

rificing, more eager, more giving, than can honestly be said to be connoted by righteousness or goodness. It is the virtue which . . . does in its height 'cause a man to lay down his life for his friend.' It is the virtue which drives a man forth to save, to redeem, and to forgive."[1]

Suffering, renunciation and death, then, stand at the centre of the New Testament meaning of *agapē*, but they are never quite the last word that the New Testament has to say about it. The last word is not suffering but joy, not death but life. From the beginning Christianity was a religion of triumphant hope, a 'resurrection faith,' a faith rooted in the conviction that love was stronger than death, and could not be holden of death, but must rise from death to life eternal. No gospel of mere renunciation and defeat, however nobly represented, could have had in it the tremendous power of spiritual appeal which the faith of that little Christian band has ever since proved itself to possess.

III

Let us now turn to the other relationship included in the Christian fellowship of love, namely, God's love for us. The first thing that must be said is that here we have not to do with a different kind of love from that which we have been discussing but with just the same

[1] *The Old Testament and After*, pp. 209 f.

kind. The light which Christianity throws upon our duty to our fellows and upon our conception of God is one light. The New Testament teaching about God and our relations with Him is apt at first to strike us as being a very complicated and involved affair when compared with the simplicity and directness of its teaching about our duty to our fellows; and that is one reason why the Christian ethic has in our day seemed to make so much wider an appeal than the Christian theology. Yet after all there is never any doubt as to the main burden of the New Testament teaching about God: it is just that He is love. Just as the New Testament ethic is summed up in the words, "Be under no obligation to anyone except the obligation of love to one another. For he who loves his fellow men has fulfilled the law"[1]—so the New Testament *religion* is summed up in the simple saying that "God is love, and he that dwelleth in love dwelleth in God, and God in him."[2]

Moreover the analogy of the family is as prominently before the minds of the earliest Christian writers in the one case as it is in the other. Just as in the one case the first thing *agapē* means is brotherliness, so in the other case the first thing it means is fatherliness. There is no doubt at all that St. Paul regarded the name Father as "the peculiarly

[1] *Romans* xiii, 8.   [2] *I John* iv, 16.

Christian name for God."[1] Indeed the very centre of his gospel is that God is our Father and that the way is open whereby we may be received into His sonship. In such a declaration as the following he is clearly proclaiming what he takes to be the very gist of the Christian missionary message:

"As many as are led by the Spirit of God, they are sons of God. For ye have not received the spirit of bondage again unto fear; but ye have received the spirit of adoption, whereby we cry, Abba, Father. The Spirit itself beareth witness with our spirit that we are the children of God . . ."[2]

The liberating realisation which participation in the Christian fellowship thus brought to St. Paul was that God was not to be regarded in the light of a taskmaster, but rather in the light of a parent, and that we are accordingly not His slaves but His children. "Wherefore thou art no more a servant but a son."[3] The technical term (υἱοθεσία) which he uses to describe this new relationship to God that is enjoyed within the Christian fellowship is usually englished as 'adoption,' though it is a pity that we cannot find a simpler word formed, as is the Greek, from the word 'son' itself. There are two things Paul stresses about this new relation-

[1] The acknowledgement is made by Dr. McGiffert in his *God of the Early Christians*, p. 24.
[2] *Rom.* viii, 14–16.   [3] *Gal.* iv, 7.

ship. One is what might almost be called the greater *informality* of it—the readier access it gives us to the Divine Presence. In the Christian fellowship, he says in one famous passage, "we have the right of free speech (παρρησία) and access (προσαγωγή) in confidence."[1] The other is the greater *graciousness* of it in respect of our sins and failures. What Christianity has taught us here, he tells us, is that God meets us on a family rather than on a forensic basis, that His dealings with us are not legal but parental, and that therefore "we are not under the law, but under grace."[2] This means simply that what reigns at the centre of the spiritual universe is not overbearing Power, nor yet calculating Justice, but rather outgoing Love. It means that that spirit of eager, patient, forgiving, redemptive love which St. Paul had described in I Corinthians XIII is not merely an ideal pattern on which we must model our attitude to our fellows, but is enthroned in highest Heaven as the Spirit manifested by the Most High God in His dealings with us. This is the "good news" which inspires Paul to his most joyful outbursts. He had spent many years of inward unrest and self-torture, thinking all the time (if his own account be true) of God as a taskmaster, and endeavouring to win favour in His sight by a "struggling task'd morality" of perfect obedience to His laws. But now he

[1]*Eph.* iii, 12.   [2]*Rom.* vi, 14.

knows that God's favour is offered to us, and may be received by us, on quite other terms than these; or rather he knows that it is offered, not on terms at all, but, as he says, "gratis" ($\delta\omega\rho\epsilon\acute{a}\nu$)[1] and "quite apart from legality" ($\chi\omega\rho\grave{\iota}\varsigma$ $\nu\acute{o}\mu o\upsilon$)[2] out of God's sheer love and pity to all who have faith to receive it.

"But now quite apart from legality there is disclosed a divine rightness . . . that comes to all who have faith. For no distinction is drawn. All have sinned and fall short of the glory of God, yet out of his graciousness they are set right for nothing . . ."[3]

"To the man who 'works' for the reward, the reward is put down, not as a favour, but as his due; but to the man who instead of 'working' puts his trust in One who sets wrong men right, this trust is itself put down as rightness."[4]

The essence of the Christianity which St. Paul adopted in preference to the faith of his earlier days[5] was therefore this—that in the last resort God is not a just Taskmaster who rewards us according to our deserts, good for

[1]*Rom.* iii, 24.   [2]*Rom.* iii, 21.
[3]*Rom.* iii, 21-24.   [4]*Rom.* iv, 4 f.

[5]It has been claimed by some recent authorities on Judaism, such as Abrahams, Montefiore, G. F. Moore and R. Travers Herford, that in his references to the faith of his earlier days Paul is not really doing justice to Judaism at its best. With this question (on which there is much that might be said) I am not here directly concerned: I am concerned rather to determine the essential nature of Christianity than to gauge the precise measure of its difference from Judaism.

good and evil for evil, but a tender-hearted Parent whose first and only thought is to redeem us from the power of sin, and who trusts in the countervailing power of His own love to work this redemption in the hearts of all who have faith to receive it.[1] But now, just as St. Paul believed that our human love cannot be effectively redemptive in the lives of our fellow men unless it be a suffering love, so he believed that the redeeming love of God must in some way also involve suffering. If our little human enterprises of redemption are costly to us, he would argue, how much more costly must be the enterprise of world-redemption to the infinite and holy God! It is this thought that forms the cope-stone, not only of the teaching of St. Paul, but of the whole Christian preaching in its New Testament form. "In this was manifested the love of God toward us . . ."—it is a form of sentence employed by more than one New Testament writer; but it is always completed by a phrase that points to some kind of divine participation in the sorrows of earth. "No God, or Absolute,"—so a modern writer has interpreted it—"existing in solitary bliss and perfection, but a God who lives in the perpetual giving of himself, who shares the life of his finite creatures, bearing in and with them the whole burden of their finitude, their sinful

[1] For adoption and justification as the two central concepts of Paul's thought see J. Weiss, *Das Urchristentum*, pp. 384-391.

wanderings and sorrows, and the suffering without which they cannot be made perfect."[1]

This, then, is the crux of the Christian message—that behind the cruelty of circumstance and behind the heart's despairing battle with itself there stands eternally a Love that suffers for our sakes. And yet just as the last word about human love is not the tragedy of suffering but the triumphant joy and peace of eternal life, so is there not a sense in which the last word about the love of God is not suffering but rather the unchanging serenity of eternal perfection? In the last resort, and each in his different manner, every New Testament writer looks beyond even the crucial fact of a divine participation in our human sorrows to that further possibility of a human participation in the everlasting divine joy, a peace of God which passeth all understanding and before which the last remaining shadow of sorrow and suffering must flee away.

IV

And now has everything been said? In a sense perhaps it has. I have done the best I can to define for you the essence of that fellowship of Christian love which was first enjoyed by the little band in the upper room at Jerusalem and from there went out to cast its spell upon the world. Such definition must necessarily be by

[1] A. S. Pringle-Pattison, *The Idea of God*, p. 411.

means of general terms and abstract nouns, and the abstract nouns which I have used have in every case been those suggested by the New Testament writers themselves—*koinōnia* and *agapē*, fatherhood and sonship and brotherhood, redemption, adoption, forgiveness, free grace and the rest. I do not know what else I ought to add. And yet I am sure that none of you are satisfied.

Why then are you dissatisfied? It is not, I believe, because my abstract nouns have not been the right ones, or because I have not used enough of them, but because the fellowship of Christian love is such a thing that no abstract nouns can ever give us more than a pale reflection of its radiant reality and living glory.

How then are we to come by a fuller understanding of it? It is to this question that we must next address ourselves.

CHAPTER IV

CHRIST THE FOUNDER

I

IN the last chapter we did our best to distil into such general terms as we found ready to our hand in the New Testament literature the essence of that new spirit which animated the little band of the first Christians, that new fellowship which they enjoyed with one another and with God.

But there was one question we did not raise. We did not ask where the new spirit had come from, or how the fellowship had suddenly sprung into being. The answer to this question at once introduces us to a figure that has all the time been standing behind the little group and its life—the figure of Jesus of Nazareth.

Jesus of Nazareth is the explanation of it all! The new spirit was just *His* spirit. The new outlook was *His* outlook. The 'Way' was *His* way. And that *agapē* which was the substance of the fellowship, what else was it but the temper that was in Him in the days of His flesh?

Now this does not mean merely that Jesus was to these early Christians an illustration of what they meant by *agapē*. It means, on the contrary, that their conception of *agapē* was but a rough attempt to express what they found in Jesus. The truth had originally come to them not through abstract thinking but through contact with a living personality, and they felt that not all the thinking they would ever be able to do could exhaust its many-sided richness and depth. Surely they were right. Surely a spiritual influence is in its very nature an inexhaustible thing. It is in the individual, not in the general, that the fulness of reality resides. No generic or abstract terms can ever quite tell you all that is meant by the spirit of St. Francis or of Garibaldi or of the Sadhu Sundar Singh. You can understand a great man's spirit only by hearing how he faced life in this and that particular situation, by acquainting yourself with as much as possible of what he did and said, and not least by observing the kind of mark he made upon the lives of those who knew him. So the New Testament writers, while making many brave attempts to analyse the spirit of their fellowship, never show the least disposition to allow such analyses to take the place of the all-controlling central reference to the spirit of Christ. If we ask Paul what *agapē* is, he will write us the thirteenth chapter of First Corinthians, but in the end he will prefer to say that it is "the mind which was in Christ Jesus." If we ask John, he too will tell us much about the workings of love, but in the end he will say only that "We know what love is by this, that he laid down his life for us; so we ought to lay down our lives for the brotherhood."[1]

The comprehensive and organic nature of this reference of the Christian religion to its concrete source in the spirit of Jesus cannot really be exaggerated. We see it first in the ethical part of the early Church's teaching, where the one all-inclusive ideal is that men should have in them the spirit of Christ, that they should follow in His 'Way,'[2] that they should manifest in their lives the temper which He manifested in His life and set forth in His advice to His followers—in a word, that "Christ should be formed in their hearts." And this is nowhere more strikingly the case than at what we have described as the summit of the Christian Way —that lonely peak of self-sacrifice and vicarious suffering. The New Testament, indeed, hardly attempts any abstract name for this highest manifestation of the Christian spirit; it is content with a concrete one—the spirit of the *Cross*. This, we are told, is what redemptive and suffering love means—that Christ died for our sakes upon a Cross of shame! "I am suffering now for your sakes," St. Paul tells the Colossians, "and I am glad I am. I am ready to make

[1]Moffatt's translation of *I John* iii, 16.
[2]One of the earliest Christian names for Christianity was "The Way."

up the deficit of Christ's sufferings for the sake
of his Body, the Community."[1] And what is
true of Christian duty is true also of Christian
hope—the hope that looks through suffering
and death to a fuller life beyond. All that the
New Testament has to say about eternal life
centres in the deep conviction that such an one
as Jesus could not be, and that in fact Jesus
had not been, holden of death. "If we have
died with him, we shall also live with him"—so
ran one of those 'reliable sayings' (πιστοὶ λόγοι)
which were current in the early Church and
are occasionally quoted in the New Testament.[2]
"If we have grown into him by a death like
his," says St. Paul, "we shall grow into him
by a resurrection like his," and again, "We
share his sufferings in order to share his glory."[3]
And to St. Paul's deeper vision this immortal
life in Christ was not merely a thing of the
future but could be presently enjoyed. "If ye
then be risen with Christ," we find him plead-
ing, "seek those things which are above."[4]

"It is one of the great principles of Christianity," says Pascal, "that all that happened to
Jesus Christ must fulfil itself in the spirit and
in the body of every Christian."

But the reference to the spirit of Jesus

[1] *Col.* i, 24.
[2] See *II Tim.* ii, 11; quoted also by St. Paul in *Rom.* vi, 8.
[3] *Rom.* vi, 5 and viii, 17: Moffatt's translation.
[4] *Col.* iii, 1.

is equally determinative in the case of the Church's teaching about God. In all that the New Testament has to say about God there is remarkably little reliance upon abstract and general terms. The God of the New Testament is "God manifest in Christ." For *agapē* as it is in God, no less than as it ought to be in man, we are referred to the mind that was in Christ Jesus. Christ is the "image" ($\epsilon i \kappa \omega \nu$)[1] or the "impress" ($\chi \alpha \rho \alpha \kappa \tau \eta \rho$)[2] of that Deity whom no man hath seen at any time. The general New Testament disposition to place its sole reliance upon the light cast on God's dealings with us by the events of Jesus' career is accurately mirrored in St. Paul's determination to know nothing among the Corinthians save Jesus Christ and Him crucified.[3] And just as Christ's bearing of His Cross holds in it the highest secret of our human relationships with one another, so also it holds in it the highest truth about God. The Cross is the shewing forth of the divine redeeming love. "God proves his love for us by this," writes St. Paul, "that Christ died . . ."[4]

II

Now it is our business in these chapters to study carefully this fact of Christianity's all-

[1] *Cf. II Cor.* iv, 4; *Col.* i, 15.
[2] *Cf. Heb.* i, 3.   [3] See *I Cor.* ii, 2.
[4] *Rom.* v, 8: Moffatt's translation.

pervading reference to the figure of Jesus and
to see what exactly it amounts to. What precisely is the nature of the relationship which is
here implied to exist between Jesus of Nazareth
and the life of the Christian Church?

Our final answer will be that the relationship
is in some sort a double one. There is a simpler,
and there is also a deeper, significance which
Jesus has always had for the brotherhood of His
followers, and each is in its own way entirely
vital. In a later chapter we shall discuss what I
have called the deeper significance. In the present chapter we shall confine ourselves to the simpler one.

The primary relationship in which Jesus
stands to the Christian fellowship is just that
He was its Founder. It is from this fact that
the New Testament Christology sets out. Perhaps the most striking term it employs in this
connection is *archēgos*. The importance of the
term is unfortunately obscured in the Authorised Version by its being given different English renderings in different places: sometimes it
is rendered as 'prince,' sometimes as 'author,'
sometimes as 'captain.' Dr. Moffatt renders it
in every case by the word 'pioneer,' and his
choice is a particularly happy one. To the early
Christians Jesus of Nazareth was the Pioneer
of the Christian 'Way'—the Pioneer of their
"life,"[1] as St. Peter said in his speech in Solo-

[1] *Acts* iii, 15.

mon's Porch, and of their "faith"[1] and their
"salvation,"[2] as the author of the *Epistle to the
Hebrews* expresses it in different contexts. In
another set of passages Jesus is very similarly
referred to as "the first-born of the Christian
brotherhood"[3]—a phraseology which led to the
later designation of "the Elder Brother."
Closely connected with this way of speaking is
St. Paul's characteristic claim that Christians,
in being heirs rather than slaves of God, are at
the same time "joint-heirs with Christ."[4] There
is in all this the constant and most vivid remembrance that it is to the spiritual vision of Jesus
of Nazareth that we owe our whole Christian
insight into the things of God and our whole
Christian discovery of the true 'Way' of life.
The primary significance of Jesus for the Christian world is just that He was the first Christian,
the Founder and first member of the fellowship
of Christian love, the first man to regard his
fellows in the true and complete spirit of
Christian brotherhood and to look up to God
as Father in quite the Christian way.

Now this means, to begin with, that we who
follow the Christian Way must look back to
Jesus as our Teacher and must look upon our-

[1] *Heb.* xii, 2.

[2] *Heb.* ii, 10. *Cf.* St. Peter in *Acts* v, 31.

[3] So St. Paul in *Rom.* viii, 29: with which compare *Heb.* i, 6;
Col. i, 15, 18; *Rev.* i, 5.

[4] *Rom.* viii, 17. *Cf. Gal.* iv, 7.

selves as His pupils. There are some people
who would deprecate such an attempt to regard Jesus in the light of a teacher, but I cannot think that in taking this attitude they are
true to the Christian tradition. No reader of the
Gospel narratives can fail to see that Jesus was
a teacher first and foremost. Those who followed Him in the days of His flesh all ad-
dressed Him simply as 'Teacher' and spoke of
themselves simply as 'pupils.' (The Authorised Version says 'master' and 'disciple,' but
these are only the Elizabethan equivalents for
what we now more commonly call 'teacher'
and 'pupil.') And the *Acts of the Apostles*
makes it plain that this was the regular usage in
the early days of the Church after Jesus' death.
The twelve who had been directly taught by
Jesus were known or remembered as 'the
twelve pupils' in a special sense, but in that
first age those who had received His teaching
only at second-hand liked to call themselves
His 'pupils' too.[1] And it is to my mind very
important that we should still continue to regard ourselves as being in the first instance just
pupils of Jesus our Master. Our first duty is to
follow the way of life pointed out to us by
Him, and until this duty is recognised, all
Christology is meaningless. "Why call ye me
'Lord, Lord,'" He said Himself, "and do not

[1] *Cf.* Harnack, *Mission and Expansion of Christianity*, Eng. tr.,
vol. II, pp. 2 ff.

the things which I say?"[1] This does not mean that these early Christians took, or that we to-day are to take, the individual remembered say-ings of Jesus as constituting a code to which our actions must directly conform. The New Testa-ment appeal is, on the contrary, much more to the *spirit* of the Master than to the particular precepts that fell from His lips; though there is no doubt a certain difference in this respect between the Gospels and the Epistles. In the Gospels the individual precepts are faithfully recorded, showing that their importance was al-ways sufficiently understood. But one of the things which have often perplexed readers of the Epistles is the almost total absence from their pages of direct quotation from the Master's teaching. Yet the deepest reason for this is that the spirit of Jesus was still so effectively alive in that circle of His first followers that there was no *need* to be always harking back to the details of its original manifestation.[2] We might almost say that when a community is found staking everything on a meticulous reference to the individual sayings and doings of its founder, it is a sign that his living spirit is be-ginning to desert them; and we might also say that the brief and imperfect record of Jesus'

[1] *Luke* vi, 46.
[2] *Cf.* E. F. Scott, *The First Age of Christianity*, p. 204. The sec-tion of J. Weiss's *Das Urchristentum* entitled "Das Leben nach den Worten des Herrn" (pp. 56–59) is worth consulting.

sayings and doings which history has preserved
to us would lose the greater part of their significance for us to-day, if we ourselves had no
such experience of the continued presence of the
spirit of Jesus in His community as might help
us to interpret them. The history of the early
Christian Church never leaves upon us the impression that its members were living in the
past, feeding themselves on the mere memory
of a departed glory. No, these men were living
in the present, enjoying an experience that was
daily renewing itself, daily growing richer and
more wonderful. That is the whole meaning of
their doctrine of the Holy Spirit. "He will take
of the things that are mine"—so the Fourth
Evangelist pictures Jesus as saying with reference to the Spirit's operation in future days—
"and will show them unto you."[1] As a contemporary writer has well expressed it, "The truly
Christian life is a life not transcribed from the
pages of the Gospels, but continuous with the
divinely human life there portrayed, because
the genius of the same Artist is at work on the
new canvas."[2]

In that higher way of teaching, then,—the

[1] *John* xvi, 15.
[2] C. H. Dodd, *The Meaning of Paul for Today* (1920), p. 130.
Cf. O. C. Quick, *Liberalism, Modernism and Tradition*, p. 92:
"If the New Testament records be at all substantially correct,
what we see in them is the progressive actualization and interpretation of a teacher's ideas through the continued operation of His
living Spirit in the society of His followers."

way which is concerned not to prescribe a new code but to suggest a new outlook—Jesus Christ is our Teacher and we are His pupils. Yet nothing is more certain than that this category of teacher and taught does not in itself exhaust the relationship in which the Founder of the Christian religion stands to those who call themselves by His name. Jesus Christ was far more than a teacher.

Even a man like Socrates was far more than a teacher. It is possible that the category of teacher and taught may be sufficient to express the relation in which certain philosophers of the more narrowly technical type have stood towards the 'schools' they founded, but quite other categories are needed in a case like that of Socrates. Like Jesus, Socrates left no writing behind him, and it is, as a matter of fact, much more difficult to feel certain about any words actually spoken by him than it is to feel certain about the words actually spoken by our Lord; yet his hold upon the thought and life of succeeding generations was greater than that of any other man whose name is mentioned in our histories of philosophy. The schools which drew their inspiration from him—the Cynics, the Cyrenaics, the Megarians, the Academy and, later on, the Lyceum and the Stoa—were more at odds about correct doctrine than have been the schools of Christian theology, yet they were all as much at one in their attachment to Socrates as have

been our theological schools in their attachment
to Jesus Christ. And the reason was that what
they found in Socrates was something much big-
ger and ampler than any mere teaching: it was a
life. It is recorded by Diogenes Laertes that An-
tisthenes, the founder of the Cynic school, used
to define virtue to his disciples as consisting in
what he called "Socratic strength" (Σωκρατικὴ
ἰσχύς).[1] "Live like Socrates" was apparently
the most effective practical advice he could give
them. And of course, just as in the case of Jesus
Christ, when men thus spoke of the spirit and
example of Socrates, it was almost more of the
manner of his dying they were thinking than of
the manner of his living. And as for ourselves,
we are still quarrelling over Socrates' teaching,
but we are all silent, and all united, as we read
in the great *Phædo* and *Apology* the story of his
death. Verily here is one who by his death has
slain more Philistines, and done more damage
to Philistinism than in all his life!

If this is true of Socrates the philosopher, it
is still more clearly true of the founders of the
great religious movements known to history.
Observers of the religious life of the Buddhist
East have often remarked on the extent to which
the imagination of the people is dominated,
not merely by the great complex of Buddhist
thought, but by the actual historical figure of
Gautama himself. As it has been put, "It is Gau-

[1] Diog. Laert., vii, 11.

tama Buddha, not the Sankhya philosophy, that is the 'Light of Asia.' "[1] Yet on the other hand it has been strongly felt that in the case of Buddhism this precedence of personality over doctrine has developed rather in spite of, than in accordance with, the native genius of the movement. Buddhism started with a negation of personality, whether human or divine, and the reverence which, in the later Mahayana form of it, has been felt for Gautama's person, is contrary to the original spirit of the system. At all events it is quite certain that the tendency of deep religious feeling to centre itself rather in the spiritual amplitude of a living personality than in a rigidly conceptualised principle or formula has in Christianity reached a climax for which no complete parallel can be found either in Buddhism or anywhere else in the world's religious history. There is a real perception of fact behind the following pronouncement of Prof. Whitehead:

"In the Sermon on the Mount, in the Parables, and in their accounts of Christ, the Gospels exhibit a tremendous fact. The doctrine may, or may not, lie on the surface. But what is primary is the religious fact. The Buddha left a tremendous doctrine. The historical facts about him are secondary to the doctrine. . . .

"Buddhism and Christianity find their origins respectively in two inspired moments of history: the life

[1] J. H. Muirhead in *Christianity and the Present Moral Unrest* (London, 1926), p. 29.

of Buddha and the life of Christ. The Buddha gave his doctrine to enlighten the world: Christ gave his life. It is for Christians to discern the doctrine. Perhaps in the end the most valuable part of the doctrine of the Buddha is its interpretation of his life."[1]

It is plain, then, that the reference of the Christian fellowship can never be merely to the teaching of Jesus, but must also be to His life and to His death. Jesus is not only His community's Teacher, He is the Life from which its life proceeds. The Gospels tell us both of His life and of His teaching, but every reader must feel that the Life is the concrete, comprehensive reality of which the Teaching, taken by itself, is only an abstracted part. "The Gospel," writes Dr. L. P. Jacks, "is neither a sermon nor a treatise on religion; but a *story*, which tells how Christianity began in something that happened, in a deed that was done, in a life that was lived. . . . Something to talk about, something worth talking about, was furnished, before the talking began."[2]

III

Such then seem to be the implications of this primary reference which the Christian religion has always had to the person of its Founder.

[1] *Religion in the Making*, pp. 51 and 55–56 of the American edition. An important earlier discussion of the matter will be found in Ritschl's *Rechtfertigung und Versöhnung*, vol. III, § 44.

[2] *Religious Perplexities*, pp. 87 f.

And we can understand why such a reference should from the beginning have been regarded as vital to the continued existence of the new faith. But now there is a difficulty which suggests itself to many contemporary minds just at this point. The advantages of having our spiritual aspirations definitely focussed in a concrete historical memory and in loyalty to a single historical figure are fully recognized and admitted, but a certain disadvantage is found in it too. It has undoubtedly a vitalising effect on our faith, but it is held also to have a narrowing one. When we are interrogated concerning the precise nature of this Christianity of ours, it is a tremendous relief to be able to escape from the perplexities of definition *per genus et differentiam* by simply pointing to a particular chapter in history, to a life that was lived and a death that was died, and saying that Christianity is *that*. On a creed we shall never again agree, but we are all agreed, and all one, in "personal loyalty and devotion to Jesus Christ"; and if that is the real essence of the Christian religion, our modern perplexities of belief are very much lightened. Yet it is felt that while the hope of a *rapprochement* between the various sects within Christianity is thus brought nearer, the hope of any *rapprochement* between Christianity and its rival religious systems is put further off than ever; and that while the acceptance of Christianity by those born and nurtured within the

Christian tradition is made easier, its acceptance by those whose native associations are with a rival tradition is made much more difficult.

Take, for instance, a city like New York, the spiritual life of which is divided between two traditions, Judaism and Christianity. There are many signs there that Jew and Christian are not as bitterly opposed to one another as they once were. Many characteristic elements of the Christian outlook have soaked themselves into much current Judaism, as indeed must have inevitably happened with any body of people living as loyal citizens within a Christian civilisation; and many find reason for hope that such Judaism may gradually become more and more Christian in temper, until at last it is more Christian than it is anything else. Yet it is felt that the one thing Jews will *never* do is to allow their devotion to centre itself in loyalty to the figure of the Nazarene. They will do anything but that. What they find good in Christian teaching they will acknowledge to be good, and they will no longer wish to exclude it as foreign and corrupt; but they will naturally be desirous of showing that it is essentially in line with the traditions of their own past, and not radically different from this and that which may be found in their own literature. Many of them will even acknowledge the essential preciousness of the teaching of Jesus Christ; but they will claim that they value Him not as the founder

of a new tradition but as one of their own prophets, and that what was truest in His teaching is
not always what was newest. But the one thing
that utterly alienates them and renders the hope
of a further *rapprochement* impossible is the
proposal of anything like 'Christocentricity'—
anything like a comprehensive focussing of religious loyalty on the one figure of the Christ.
That, precisely, is the *skandalon*, the stone of
stumbling, the rock of offence. Tell us, they will
say, what ideals of life and beliefs about God
your Christianity stands for, and perhaps we
shall find that they are hardly different from
those of our own Judaism—perhaps we can accept them almost as they stand. But to say that
Christianity is nothing but personal devotion
to Jesus Christ—that is to set the traditional
stumbling-block right before our feet, and to
state your faith in the one way that we can never
make our own.

There is here, surely, a living problem. And
it is a problem which is not confined to the case
of the Jews. It emerges in largely the same form
in our Christian contacts with Islam, which,
though treasuring the memory both of Moses
and of Jesus, yet centres its traditional loyalty in
the figure of Mohammed. It emerges also in
the experience of many of the missionaries who
work among modern Hindus. Unquestionably
modern Hinduism has appropriated to itself
many Christian ideas, and not a few young

Hindus are now conscious of this debt and even eager to increase it, but the suggestion that they should substitute personal loyalty to Jesus Christ for the whole native framework of their own Indian religion causes difficulty of a very different kind.

Is it then our Christian duty to cease to focus our religious life upon the figure of our Lord, and to make our Christianity stand rather for a body of principles that may be detached from a historical and personal context which has proved a *skandalon* to so many of our human brothers? We cannot believe that it is.

That there is an important element of truth in the view just sketched I should be very ready to allow. There is a certain kind of 'Christocentricity' in the interpretation of the Christian faith which may easily overreach itself, and has often done so. It is quite possible to state the essence of Christianity in such a way as to obscure what it has in common with other religious traditions and to exaggerate the breach which it makes with them. This was the mistake made by Marcion in the second century and it is a mistake which a misdirected zeal for the universal acknowledgement of Christ's supremacy has led some of our own contemporaries to repeat. The New Testament writers, as we saw, though never willing in the last resort to make their Christianity anything else than a living loyalty to their Master, yet make the most resolute attempts to analyse the content of this loyalty and to set out in general terms its implications for daily life and for our idea of God. We are told not only that we must have in us the spirit of Christ, we are told also what the spirit of Christ is. When the meaning of Christianity is thus temporarily released from its concrete embodiment in a particular personality and chapter of events, and caught up into abstract terms, it becomes possible to compare it with other religious systems, to see just what it has in common with them and where it goes beyond them. And so we are enabled to do justice to other and rival traditions, and a door is opened to a real measure of fellowship with those who do not know, or who will not acknowledge, the name of Christ —with Jew and Mohammedan and Hindu; while at the same time we are making it easier for these to embark upon the perilous spiritual adventure to which our missionaries call them. There is here an immensely important service which we can render to the spiritual life of the world, and it is our duty to-day to spare no effort towards its furtherance. We have had more than enough of religious bickerings and misunderstandings, of hard-shelled exclusivisms, of uninstructed prejudices doggedly surviving from age to age. We are almost as tired of the old head-on collisions between Christian and Jew, or between Christian and 'Saracen,' as we are of the old head-on collisions between the

various Christian sects. And we have our doubts
as to whether the evangelisation of the world
can ever be accomplished until we have put more
intelligence into our missionary approach than
we have commonly put into it in the past.

It is our duty then, in this day and generation,
to do our best to arrive at such a presentation of
our Christian religion as will make it most easy
of access to those who have been reared in other
and rival spiritual traditions. Clearly, however,
it cannot be asked of us that we should make
any change in it which would amount to a curtailment of its significance or of its power. But
it is certain that we should be guilty of just such
a curtailment if we allowed our Christianity per-
manently to detach itself from the living figure
of our Lord. It is useless to hope that a body of
principles can ever do for men what the Gospel
story has done for them. Words, words—we
grow so weary of them! The world, we feel, is
too full of talk, too full of good advice! But we
thank God that once at least the word was *made
flesh* and *dwelt among us* and we beheld its
glory!

There are indeed two distinct ways in which
the mere teaching of Christ, when taken separately, falls short of His living Self in significance and power. First, there is in the living personality and in the living deed an inexhaustible-
ness of suggestion that not even the lips of Jesus
Christ could ever have reduced to abstract for-

mulæ. And second, we men being what we are, ideas can seldom really sway our souls until they have become incarnate in a living example. How then can we hope that adherence to an abstract ethical system can ever take the place of personal devotion to a living Master, or that a "doctrine of the atonement" can ever take the place of the story of the Cross?

The deepest service we can render towards those of our fellow men whose sympathies are strongly entrenched in a rival and (as we feel) inferior religious tradition is first to discover how far they and we stand upon common ground, and then, as regards what remains, not to attempt any kind of superficial accommodation in a spirit of good-natured compliance, but rather to continue to bear our own unabridged witness to the truth as we see it. And if it appear to us that the full and characteristic benefits of the Christian faith can only be enjoyed by those who, as latter-day members of the fellowship of the Upper Room, keep their "eyes fixed upon Jesus as the pioneer and perfection of faith,"[1] then we owe it to our fellows to tell them this as clearly and persuasively as we can. Here, as so often, the facts of life are too complex and too unyielding for a weak sentimentality to be of the least service to us in facing them.

[1] *Hebrews* xii, 2.

CHAPTER V

WAS HE REALLY THE FOUNDER?

I

WE cannot go further with our argument without first pausing to consider what looks like a very serious difficulty. We have seen that the Christian brotherhood has from the beginning regarded itself as having its source in "the mind which was in Christ Jesus," and it has seemed clear to us that this organic reference of our Christian faith and life to the living figure of the Founder is a necessary condition of its continued vitality and effectiveness in the world. But of recent years a number of learned and responsible historical scholars have appeared to champion the view, in one form or another, that Jesus of Nazareth was *not*, in actual fact, the founder of the Christian religion, because what is most distinctive in its faith and life cannot be traced back to Him but originated after His death in the Pentecostal community itself or even in the mind of St. Paul.

This view is to be regarded as representing the extreme limit of a tendency in the historical criticism of the New Testament which has marked the whole modern epoch and which every competent enquirer now believes to be justified up to a certain point. Traditional theology, having been (as we now think) singularly deficient in historical sense, was unaware of any difference whatever between the teaching of Jesus and that of the apostolic age—as reflected most notably in the Epistles of St. Paul. The religion taught by Jesus and that taught by St. Paul were represented as being identical in every particular; as indeed must have been the case, seeing that both Gospels and Epistles were regarded as direct and undiluted (and perhaps even verbally accurate) messages from heaven. There was, however, a difference between the religion *practised* by Jesus and that practised by Paul, because Paul and Jesus occupied different positions in that redemptive scheme which was identically the same in the teaching of both: in that scheme Jesus was the Redeemer while Paul was but one of the redeemed. So the Christianity of the early Church was held to be more than the religion *of* Jesus, because it was also a religion *about* Jesus; but between the two there was no degree of discrepancy, because it was held that this religion *about* Jesus was the religion which Jesus Himself had taught His disciples to practise, though in the nature of the case He could not completely practise it Himself.

It is against this position that the historical scholarship of the last three-quarters of a century has entered so vigorous a protest. That this protest has been justified we are all now agreed. It is no longer possible for us to read our New Testaments without being very wide awake to the vastly different frameworks in which (to mention only that one example) are set the thinking of our Lord and the thinking of the great Apostle to the Gentiles. But a difference in framework is one thing, and a difference in essential message and intention quite another. And what is claimed by those recent writers to whom I referred at the beginning is just that the essential message for which the primitive and Pauline community is now seen to have stood cannot any longer be held to have had its real source in the mind of our Lord Himself. The religion *of* Jesus, we are now told, was one thing, while the Pauline religion *about* Jesus was quite another thing, the two being radically discrepant in many essential ways. The nature of this discrepancy is not always stated in quite the same fashion, but the extreme view may perhaps be said to be that Jesus was to all intents and purposes an orthodox Jew, with little in His teaching that was new, but with a greater than usual absorption in the apocalyptic outlook, whereas the religion that after His death grew around His name was, more than anything else, a variety of the Græco-Oriental myth of a Dying God.

Here, plainly, is a problem which we must resolutely tackle, for there is hardly any historical conclusion which could be more deeply disturbing to the life of Christian devotion, as I have tried to describe it in the two foregoing chapters, than this one which sets a gulf between our Christian faith and the mind of our Lord Himself, and cuts all deeper estimates of His significance at the root by denying Him His primary position as Founder. That most wide-awake of recent German theologians, Ernst Troeltsch, has declared this to be the most important problem now confronting us in the sphere of Christological discussion. In the opening paragraphs of the Christological section of his posthumously published *Glaubenslehre* we read as follows:

"The central problem, as it presents itself to-day, is the question whether the early community's religion of Christ and redemption is a result which arose out of the impression made by Jesus Himself and which is inwardly continuous with His Person, *or* whether this faith in a Saviour, with its focussing of redemption in the sacrificial death of a Saviour-God, is merely the grafting of non-Christian mystery-cults upon the more or less irrelevant surviving memory of a Jewish rabbi."[1]

I believe the view in question to be radically mistaken. Despite all the manifest differences of detail between the outlook reflected in the Gospels and that reflected in the Epistles, I be-

[1] *Glaubenslehre* (1925), p. 101.

lieve that at heart they are one and the same outlook, having very plainly—if we may vary the metaphor—an identical centre of gravity. And so I shall devote this chapter to an attempt to show that Jesus of Nazareth really was the Founder of Christianity and the Pioneer in all that is most distinctive in its faith and in its life.

It will be remembered that we found the essence of apostolic Christianity to consist in the experience of a divine-human fellowship in which each man stood in a relation of *agapē* towards God as Father and towards his fellow men as brothers. What I shall now try to show is that the conception and realisation of such a fellowship goes back in the fullest possible way to the spiritual insight of the historic Jesus.

II

As regards the ethical aspect of the apostolic fellowship—its conception of the love of man for man—this contention does not really stand in need of elaborate proof. It has often been remarked with reference to the Pauline Epistles that however unlike the Gospels they may be in almost every other way, yet in their ultimate pronouncements about conduct there is just no difference at all. The Apostle's thought seems often to traverse very different channels from that of His Master, but as regards the practical result of it, it always comes out at exactly the same point. Their theologies may look different, but at least their conceptions of Christian character are one and the same. Indeed the more attentively we read what St. Paul has to say about Christian character, the more do we come to feel that he is hardly doing more than painting the portrait of Jesus of Nazareth. "Love is very patient, very kind. Love knows no jealousy; love makes no parade, gives itself no airs, is never rude, never selfish, never irritated, never resentful; love is never glad when others go wrong, love is gladdened by goodness, always slow to expose, always eager to believe the best, always hopeful, always patient"—can we have any doubt who it was who sat in the studio of Paul's imagination for that famous little vignette of the ideal man? And what doubt is there that the Apostle's own *agapē*, the *agapē* which drove him to the ends of the world in missionary enterprise, went back for its one source to the remembrance of his Master's love for the poor, for the sick, for those in prison, for the lost sheep, for the prodigal sons?

Nor is it merely with the silent spirit of his Master's life that St. Paul's teaching shows a close correspondence, but also with His spoken words. There is not a phrase in that description of love which St. Paul wrote to the Corinthians that cannot be paralleled with a saying of Jesus. And we may set the long opening sentence of the same great chapter beside an equally familiar passage from the teaching of our Lord:

"I may speak with the tongues of men and of angels, but if I have no love, I am a noisy gong or a clanging cymbal; I may prophesy, fathom all mysteries and secret lore, I may have such absolute faith that I can move hills from their place, but if I have no love, I count for nothing; I may distribute all I possess in charity, I may give up my body to be burnt, but if I have no love, I make nothing of it."[1]

"So you will know them by their fruit. It is not every one who says to me 'Lord, Lord!' who will get into the Realm of heaven, but he who does the will of my Father in heaven. Many will say to me at that Day, 'Lord, Lord, did we not prophesy in your name? did we not cast out demons in your name? did we not perform many miracles in your name?' Then I will declare to them, 'I never knew you. . . .'"[2]

Is it possible not to feel how closely the first of these passages is following the second?

It will be remembered that we summed up the meaning of brotherly love, as it was understood within the apostolic fellowship, as "the transference, by an act of imaginative sympathy, to all those with whom we have to do, of those sentiments of tenderness and affection which even the meanest of us bestow upon our own flesh and blood."[3] But nothing is more certain than that this insight goes back for its inception to the mind of our Lord. It was He who first realised this deep and wide significance that is latent in family life and its sentiment of brotherliness. The distinctive Chris-

[1]Moffatt's translation.

[2]*Matt.* vii, 20–23: Moffatt's translation.

[3]See above, p. 44.

tian use of the word 'brother' is plainly of His own institution. "One is your teacher," He said to His disciples, "and all you are brothers."[1] And again, "Stretching out his hand towards his disciples, he said, Here are my mother and my brothers."[2] Indeed there is no better way of summing up His whole teaching concerning our relations with those around us than by saying that, in all our dealings with them, brotherliness is to take the place of justice. We are to put aside all that miserable machinery that we have invented for dealing with those who are outside the circle of our immediate kin, and which is the joint product of fear and jealousy and greed; we are to put aside legal justice and retributive punishment and satisfaction for wrongs inflicted and the *lex talionis* and all their wretched company; and we are to deal with all men as we would deal with our own brothers and our own sons. That is what the Christian spirit meant for Jesus, and it is also what it meant for every writer of the apostolic age.

But there was one particular implication of this Christian brotherliness which we were led to emphasise in speaking of Paul and his contemporaries, and which we must now emphasise no less in speaking of the teaching of our Lord.

---

[1] *Matt.* xxiii, 8. The occurrence of the word 'brothers' here arrests attention all the more because we expect rather 'pupils' ($\mu\alpha\theta\eta\tau\alpha\dot{\iota}$).

[2] *Matt.* xii, 49.

The spirit of brotherly love, we saw, did not merely mean that we were to be patient and forbearing and forgiving in our dealings with our fellows, it meant also that we were to go out after them in arduous redemptive enterprise. Christian love, we found, was above all things else a *redemptive* love—a love that helps, a love that saves, a love that goes out to seek the lost. But now what is there that lies nearer the centre both of the preaching and of the practice of our Lord than this insistence upon the duty of exercising our love to a redemptive end? What parable is more central to His message than the parable of the Lost Sheep? What hours spent by Him are more revealing of His heart and mind than the hours He spent among the lost sheep of the house of Israel—among the halt and maimed and blind, among the publicans and sinners, among broken men and fallen women? When John the Baptist sent two of his disciples to Jesus with the question, "Art thou he that should come, or do we look for another?" Jesus replied, "Go and show John again those things which ye do hear and see: the blind receive their sight, and the lame walk, and the lepers are cleansed, and the deaf hear, the dead are raised up, and the poor have the gospel preached to them."[1] That is Jesus' idea of Christianity. That is how He conceives of the final religion. We are to look,

[1] *Matt.* xi, 3-5.

He says, for nothing higher than that. We misunderstand Him, taking Him to mean that Christianity is attested or constituted by 'miracles.' Yet Jesus Himself always seemed to claim that there was nothing 'miraculous' about His mighty works, which were no more than might always be the natural products of a little faith and a little love—"even as a grain of mustard seed"; and He declared also that to many workers of so-called miracles He would at the last be obliged to say "I never knew you." Ah no! It was not their spectacular quality or their unaccountability that made the deeds witnessed by John's disciples so plainly premonitory of the dawn of a new era, it was the *redemptive passion* that was in them. One of the most valuable services which the Jewish writer, Dr. Claude Montefiore, has rendered to the study of the Gospels has been his generous insistence, in book after book, upon the real and epoch-making originality of this contribution which Jesus makes to the spiritual advance of mankind. The Rabbis, he says in one remarkable passage,

"welcomed the sinner in his repentance. But to *seek out* the sinner, and, instead of avoiding the bad companion, to choose him as your friend in order to work his moral redemption, this was, I fancy, something new in the religious history of Israel. . . . It was, doubtless, often a daring method; even with Jesus it may not always have been successful. But it inaugurated a new idea: the idea of redemption, the idea of giving a fresh object of love and interest to the sinner, and so freeing him from sin. The rescue and deliverance of the sinner through pity and love and personal service—the work and the method seem alike due to the teacher of Nazareth."[1]

If it be really true, as a historical fact, that the inauguration of the idea of redemption goes back to Jesus of Nazareth, and that this was the idea for which, both in His words and His deeds, He mainly stood, then the apostolic community made no great mistake in linking with His name the message they brought to "the circle of the lands."

No less clearly, however, are we able to trace back to Jesus Himself the final insight which we found to be implied in the apostolic conception of brotherly love—the thought that it cannot be effectively redemptive unless it be a *suffering* love. It might indeed be thought natural, and involved in the very nature of the case, that at this point St. Paul and his contemporaries should depend more upon the impression made upon themselves by the events of Jesus' own suffering and death than by any words that He spoke during His life. Yet in the first place, was it not the spirit in which Jesus faced these events that made so profound an impression

[1] *Some Elements of the Religious Teaching of Jesus*, pp. 57–58. I have also commented on this passage in my *Interpretation of Religion*, p. 443.

upon them, rather than the actual happening of the events themselves? And in the second place, who was it after all who had first taught them what these events imported, but just Jesus Himself? Would the disciples' faith ever have recovered from the tragedy of Calvary, would the Resurrection faith ever have been possible to them, if Jesus had not long before said "The Son of Man must first suffer, and give his life a ransom for many," and "I have a baptism to be baptized with, and how am I straitened till it be accomplished"? It is equally plain that Jesus realised the revealing light which His own experience of suffering threw upon the universal nature of all truly redemptive love. "Drink ye all of it," He said of the cup that represented His blood that was about to be shed. And even if we discount such sayings as "Greater love hath no man than this . . ." and "Except a corn of wheat . . ." as purely Johannine, and allow that the phrasing of such a saying as "Whosoever doth not bear his cross and come after me, cannot be my disciple" may bear upon it the mark of later history, yet we still have everywhere in the teaching of our Lord the same broad sentiment that no man can be His disciple who is not willing to leave father and mother and wife and children and brothers and sisters in order to the better performance of his redemptive duty. Undoubtedly our Christian discovery of the arduousness

of the redemptive enterprise goes back to the
mind that was in Christ Jesus.

"All that Christ asked of the world wherewith to save it," said Lamennais, "was a cross
whereon to die."

III

We pass now to the other and greater relationship included in the Christian *agapē*—God's
fatherly love towards us and the sense of sonship to which it gives rise in our human hearts.
Can we claim that here too the Pauline and
Johannine teaching has its essential roots in the
mind of the Master?

It is to this question particularly that a nega-
tive answer has been given by the group of contemporary historians mentioned above. Their
view is that in His conception of God and of
all God's dealings with men Jesus Himself was
an orthodox Jew, and that the distinctively
Christian view of God and His dealings is an
original product of the apostolic mind, though
some would allow it to be a product partly determined by the influence of the moral character of Jesus. "Jesus," writes Loisy, "does not
even pretend to make God known under a new
aspect."[1] There is no sign, writes Prof. Lake,
"that Jesus felt that he had any new revelation
as to the nature of God."[2] "The God of Jesus

[1] *L'Évangile et l'Église*, Ch. III.
[2] *Landmarks in the History of Early Christianity*, p. 62.

is the God of the Jews," he writes again in col-
laboration with Prof. Foakes-Jackson.[1] Of recent years Dr. McGiffert has seemed to be converted to this view. "The God of Jesus," he
writes, "was the God of the Jews, pure and
simple. . . . The step which he had failed to
take was taken by the apostle Paul. In his hands
the new religion became a saving cult. . . ."[2]
"So far as the God of the Christians is different
from the God of the Jews, it is due not to
Jesus' teaching about God, but to the teaching
of Paul and those that came after, or still more
to the personality of Jesus and the interpretation his followers put upon it."[3] The meaning
of all these pronouncements is clear: they mean
that the new and forward step in religion on
which the Christian Church founds is to be
placed, not between the Rabbis and Jesus, but
between Jesus and Paul.

I believe this view to be demonstrably false,
and I shall try to indicate the lines on which a
demonstration of its falsity may proceed.

The heart of the Johannine gospel is that
"God is love." The heart of the Pauline gospel
is that God is not a taskmaster who rewards us
in strict proportion as we obey His rules, but a
Father who, while we are still disobedient to
His rules, seeks us out in love and accepts us

[1]*The Beginnings of Christianity*, vol. I, p. 288.
[2]*The God of the Early Christians*, p. 193.
[3]*Ibid.*, p. 21.

into His fellowship of His own free grace. But it is not difficult to show that this great and emancipating conception of Deity not only had its ultimate source in that enhanced conception of brotherly love and forgiveness which Jesus preached and practised as regards our man-to-man relations, but had also its proximate source in Jesus' own application of this new ethical insight to the thought of God the Father. It has always seemed to me that the burden of proof in this matter lies, not with those who affirm an identity of outlook between Jesus and His disciples, but with those who deny such an identity; for how the new religion could have grown out of devotion to the memory of one who was no more than a staunch supporter of the old would in itself be a fact loudly calling for satisfactory explanation. Now it is denied by all the historians mentioned above that our Lord placed any greater emphasis on the thought of God's fatherhood than was placed on it by other Jews of His day. Yet that *Paul* thought of Christianity as placing a new and peculiar emphasis on this thought is, as we saw in an earlier chapter,[1] not denied by anybody. There is therefore a strong initial presumption in favour of the view that this emphasis had its source in the mind of Paul's Lord; and this presumption is, as I believe, sufficient to weigh down the scale of the Synoptic evidence on the

[1]See above, pp. 48 f.

matter until it becomes nothing less than certainty. As to this Synoptic evidence I shall content myself with setting down the testimony of two contemporary Jews, which, though it may not go far, goes quite far enough to prove my point. Rabbi Joseph Klausner of Jerusalem writes as follows:

"The phrase 'Our Father, who art in heaven' is so common in the *Talmudic* literature as to render quotation superfluous. . . . In this also Jesus is a genuine Jew. Jesus, however, makes far more use of such expressions as 'Father,' 'My Father,' 'My Father in heaven' than do the Pharisees and *Tannaim*; and often when he employs it, it receives an *excessive* emphasis."[1]

And he goes on to speak of Jesus' "*exaggerated* sense of nearness to God." The other writer is Dr. Montefiore, who says:

"We certainly do not get in the Hebrew Bible any teacher speaking of God as 'Father,' 'my Father,' 'your Father,' and 'our Father' like the Jesus of Matthew. We do not get so habitual and concentrated a use from any Rabbi in the Talmud. And this habitual and concentrated use rightly produces upon us an impression."[2]

[1] *Jesus of Nazareth*, American edition (1925), pp. 377 f.

[2] *The Old Testament and After*, p. 205. It is rather amusing to find Dr. Montefiore administering a gentle rebuke to Professors Foakes-Jackson and Lake for their exaggerated negations on this point. He quotes, "The fatherhood of God is a characteristically Jewish doctrine, found in equal abundance in the Old Testament and in Rabbinic literature," and he adds, "There is a little exaggeration in this sentence, at least about the Old Testament" (*Loc. cit.*).

Far more decisive, however, than our Lord's
use of any particular phraseology is the simple
fact that He seldom put forward His admittedly new teaching about the love of one another without in the same breath carrying the
analogy to that greater love which God bears to
us. Love, He always seems to be telling us, is
essentially the same thing in man and in God.
"After this manner therefore pray ye, . . .
Forgive . . . as we forgive . . ." And we are
not commanded even to love our enemies without being told that God loves *His* enemies.
"Love your enemies, and do good, and lend,
hoping for nothing again . . . and ye shall be
the children of the Most High: for he is kind
to the unthankful and the evil. Be ye therefore
merciful, as your Father is also merciful."[1]
After all, how identical that is with Paul's essential gospel! It was Jesus, not Paul, who first
clearly declared what the prophets and psalm-
ists of Israel had long ago begun to understand
—that justice and law are not God's last words
in His dealings with men. It was Jesus, not
Paul, who first told us that God is not a taskmaster who loves only righteous men and rewards them in proportion as they have succeeded in keeping his rules, but is rather a
Lover who seeks us out while we are yet sinners and bestows His gifts of His own free grace.
It was Jesus, not Paul, who first told us that

[1] *Luke* vi, 35–36.

there is more joy in God's heart over one sinner that repenteth than over ninety and nine just persons, which need no repentance. It was Jesus who first in a parable made God say, "I will grant unto this last even as unto thee. Is it not lawful for me to do what I will with mine own? Dost thou look with envy, because I am generous? So the last shall be first, and the first last."[1] And how essentially (even after we have discounted Luke's use of the word 'justify' as being possibly due to Paul's own influence) is the Pauline gospel of salvation not by works but by grace through faith contained in Jesus' parable of the Pharisee and the publican, with its cry of "God be merciful to me a sinner" and its conclusion that "this man went down to his house justified rather than the other"![2]

There is, in fact, no historical perception which is more necessary to the proper understanding of the New Testament than the perception that the characteristic outlook of Paulinism has its roots firmly planted in this distinction on which Jesus was always insisting between two ways of facing life and approaching the Divine—the way of the Pharisee and the way of the publican in the parable. The distinction finds its first clear expression in the Beatitudes, where blessedness is promised only to those who are "poor in spirit" and "meek" and who "hunger

[1]*Matt.* xx, 13–16; one phrase is from Moffatt's translation.
[2]*Luke* xviii, 13–14.

and thirst after righteousness." It reaches its height in the selection of the little child as furnishing a type for the attitude of mind necessary for entrance into the privileges of the divine fellowship. "Of such is the Kingdom of God. Verily I say unto you, Whosoever shall not receive the Kingdom of God as a little child, he shall not enter therein."[1] What God requires of us as a precondition of acceptance into the kingdom of His love is not—so our Lord consistently taught—any kind of attainment, but only humility. It does not matter if we have nothing to *offer*, so long as only we are willing to *receive*. For Jesus, as for Paul, God's Kingdom is always a free *gift*. "It is your Father's good pleasure to give you the Kingdom."[2] It is worth while to quote the testimony of the same two Jewish writers, Montefiore and Klausner, on this point. The former writes:

"The Kingdom . . . is not so much a reward as a grace. Do what he will, man never deserves it; do his duty as he may, man has no claim for special recognition and reward. The Kingdom, when it comes, will be far greater and more glorious than any man can have merited. It is not the product of calculating justice and retribution; it is the outflow of God's free and exuberant love.

I do not think that these few statements go beyond what Jesus actually says in the Synoptic Gospels, and I am also inclined to think that, though they are not

[1]*Mark* x, 14-15. [2]*Luke* xii, 32.

without their parallels in the Rabbinic literature, they nevertheless may be regarded as comparatively new and original."[1]

Rabbi Klausner is still more emphatic in his attribution to Jesus of the teaching that our acceptance with God is in no way preconditioned by any merit on our part, but it is interesting to see that, unlike Dr. Montefiore, he utterly rejects this teaching as contravening the spirit of Judaism:

"There was yet another element in Jesus' idea of God which Judaism could not accept.

Jesus tells his disciples that they must love their enemies as well as their friends, since their 'Father in heaven makes his sun to rise on the evil and on the good, and sends his rain upon the righteous and upon the ungodly.' . . . It follows, therefore, that God is not *absolute righteousness*, but *the good* before whom is no evil. . . . He is not the God of justice, in spite of his Day of Judgement: in other words, *he is not the God of History*.

With this, Jesus introduces something new into the idea of God. . . . Not that Judaism does not also rate highly the repentant sinners. . . . But the unrepentant *destroy the world*, they break down the *moral* order, and therefore destroy the *natural* order too. . . . God is good; but he also requires justice. He is 'merciful and compassionate, long-suffering and of great kindness'; but, none the less, 'he will by no means acquit the guilty.' . . . Jesus' idea of God is the very reverse."[2]

[1] *Some Elements of the Religious Teaching of Jesus*, pp. 97 f.
[2] *Jesus of Nazareth*, pp. 379 f.

The assumption is constantly being made by writers of our day that the redemptive aspect of the Christian religion is purely Pauline in origin, and does not go back at all to the Jesus of the Synoptic narratives. Nothing could be less true. We have already seen how Jesus' own ministry was entirely given over to the enterprise of redemption. All His days were spent in going out after the lost sheep of His native land and seeking to win them back into the fold. And when people twitted Him about the strange company He was thus led to keep, His deliberate reply was, "I have not come to call just men but sinners."[1] Yet no attentive reader of the Gospels can fail to be aware that He goes to these lost sheep armed, not merely with His own love, but with the love of Almighty God. He seeks them out Himself, but His essential message to them is that God is seeking them out. "The Pharisees and scribes murmured, saying, This man receiveth sinners and eateth with them"[2]; and Jesus, to justify this redemptive passion of His, told them the parables of the lost sheep, the lost coin and the lost son; yet when He has finished telling them, it is only God's redemptive passion that He justifies! He does not say that likewise there is more joy in His own human heart over one repentant sinner than over ninety and nine just

[1] *Matt.* ix, 13: Moffatt's translation.
[2] *Luke* xv, 2.

persons; He says that there is more joy in
heaven—in the heart of God. And what is that
but the gospel of redemption——

> "The patience of immortal love
> Outwearying mortal sin."[1]

In speaking of the religion of the apostolic
age we found its crowning insight to be the
realisation that the divine redemptive quest of
the human heart somehow necessarily involves
suffering, and that such suffering found its supreme embodiment in the Passion and death of
Christ. There is a sense, no doubt, in which this
teaching had to wait for the Master's death before finding expression. God could not be found
in the Crucifixion until the Crucifixion had
taken place. And in this respect, if in no other,
it is true that the Christianity of the apostolic
age represents a fuller gospel than any that
could have come from the Master's own lips in
the days of His flesh. So it might be held that
instead of claiming that Jesus anticipated Paul
in finding in His Passion a revelation of the
suffering love of God, we must content ourselves with claiming, in the words of Archbishop Temple, that "His bearing throughout
the Passion is the exact counterpart of His own
teaching about God."[2] Yet this is not quite the
whole truth. It is plain that, in looking forwards

[1] Whittier, "My Birthday."
[2] In *Foundations* (ed. Streeter), p. 221.

to His own death, He found in it a divine—we might almost say a cosmic—significance. He knew Himself to have been chosen of God for this work of redeeming Israel's lost sheep, and He knew also that His suffering and death were a divinely-appointed part of this work of redemption. And so in His forward view of it, hardly less definitely than in Paul's backward view, the Cross appeared as the final seal and proof of God's love for man.[1]

But here, as we reach the limits of our present subject, there comes into view that deeper aspect of our Lord's significance for His Church's life which is to occupy us in the next chapter.

IV

Meanwhile I think that we have fully established the Church's right to what we called the simpler view of its Lord's significance—His significance as the true Pioneer of its faith and Founder of its fellowship. I believe, indeed, that this side of Jesus' significance is clearer to us now than it has ever been before. That new feeling for the actualities of history which has come to our Western World during the last hundred years has resulted in our now having in our possession a truer picture of the Jesus of history than has been available to any previous

[1]One of the best statements on this whole matter is in Paul Feine's *Jesus Christus und Paulus* (1902), pp. 268–276.

generation of Christians since the apostolic age; and here we have, beyond question, one of the greatest gains—perhaps the very greatest—which the mind of our time has had to contribute to the further development of our Christian heritage. It is but too true that this century-long 'quest of the historical Jesus' has had its perplexities, its set-backs, and even its moments of despair. But for myself I have no doubt at all that it has left us richer than it found us. It has brought our Lord far closer to our latter-day souls and to our latter-day problems than He could ever otherwise have been. It has given us a Brother of the very kind we need, one tempted and tried in the very ways in which life tries and tempts ourselves, yet victorious over life and showing us the way to victory. Never before has it been quite so true that His life was the light of men.

Of recent years there has been a tendency among a certain school of writers, who have combined a 'modernist' open-mindedness towards the historical criticism of the Gospels with a close attachment to the later 'catholic' tradition, to draw a sharp contrast between the "Jesus of history" and the "Christ of faith," and to declare that their own interest is centred in the latter rather than the former. To this end they have been ready to make alliance with the school of historical writers whom we have in this chapter been concerned to criticise. They

will tell you that Jesus, so far from having
founded the Christian religion in all its fulness
and richness, was an orthodox Jew with no new
teaching of any kind. They will tell you that
the true core and centre of the Christian religion lies not in the teaching of Jesus, nor in the
spirit in which He went to His death, but
rather in the fact (which became progressively
clear and definite to the mind of the Church in
the early centuries) that it was the second person of the Divine Trinity who here lived and
died. Yet I am convinced that none of the
alternatives at present confronting Christian
thought has so little light of hope in it as this
one. No more is needed for its complete col-
lapse than the simple reminder that *if* there
was nothing remarkable in the spirit in which
Jesus faced His life or in His teaching about
how life should be faced, *then* there is left to
us no possible or thinkable ground for finding
God present in Him in any greater way or
degree than He is present in the rest of us. It
was the impression made upon His disciples by
the spirit and the words of the historic Jesus
which first suggested to them that higher view
of His significance to which the Church has
ever since clung; and it is only so far as the historic Jesus, as portrayed in the existent records,
can still make that impression upon us, that we
of to-day can hope to share that view and find
it reasonable.

Thus to the attempted separation of the religion *of* Jesus and the religion *about* Jesus there is only one effective reply. There is no hope in the position that Christianity founds not in the former but in the latter. Nor is there any hope in the position that it founds in a combination of both, regarded as different and separate entities. The only hope lies in seeing that, in the last resort, and at heart, the two religions are one and the same. I believe, and I have tried to prove, that every essential root of the religion of Paul and the apostolic age is to be found in the mind of Jesus of Nazareth. And for myself I will add this, and I will say it in full remembrance of the many puzzles and perplexities which the study of the New Testament still continues to present to me—that the light of Christian truth which has illumined for me the dark and difficult road of life nowhere shines with so clear and pure a radiance as just in the Synoptic story. Whatever may be the testimony of others, to me it still seems that neither in any earlier nor in any later teaching do we find an outlook on life suggested to us which is quite so convincingly true and right as the outlook set forth in the words and carried out in the deeds of the historic Jesus.

Carl A. Rudisill Library
LENOIR RHYNE COLLEGE

CHAPTER VI

GOD IN CHRIST

I

IN the last two chapters we have been regarding our Lord Jesus Christ in His primary significance as the Pioneer of the Christian faith. But we have all the time been aware that the brotherhood of His followers has never stopped short with this primary significance but always, building upon its foundation, has gone on to find in Him a significance of a further and deeper kind. It has looked back on that cycle of events between the Baptism and the Cross and it has seemed to find in them not merely a record of human faith but also a record of divine grace. In the advent of the Man of Nazareth, when the time was ripe, it has found not merely a gathering-together in one personality of possibilities that had long lain dormant in the history of His race, but also a direct enterprise of God for the enlightenment and salvation of the world. In the spirit of His life it has found not merely an ideal for humanity, but also the self-disclosure of Deity. And in His death upon the Cross it has found

not merely a sublime example of human mar-
tyrdom, but also the supreme declaration and
proof of the love of God for man. "In this was
manifested the love of God for us," says the
Johannine author—"God proves his love for
us by this," says St. Paul, "that Christ died
. . ."[1] And the unknown writer of the *Epistle
to Titus* quotes a 'reliable saying' current in the
apostolic age in which the advent of Jesus is
spoken of as "the epiphany of the kindness and
philanthropy (or love to man) of God our
Saviour."[2] There is no room for doubt that it is
this culminating aspect of the Gospel, more
than any other, which (to apply a phrase of
Matthew Arnold's) "has made the fortune of
Christianity" during the long period of its history. And I should find it hard to believe that
there is any one of us—no matter by what name
we call ourselves, 'fundamentalist' or 'modernist', 'Trinitarian' or 'Unitarian'—who is entirely
without the feeling that we have somehow here
to do, not only with the deepest thing in Christianity, but with a deeper thing than can anywhere else be found. "Therein," wrote St. Augustine about the Platonist books he had studied in his youth, "therein I read, not indeed
in the very words, but to the very same
purpose, that 'in the beginning was the Word.'
. . . But that 'the Word was made flesh and

[1] *I John* iv, 9; *Romans* v, 8.
[2] *Titus* iii, 4.

dwelt among us,' that I read not there."[1] "At that time," he goes on, "I conceived of my Lord Christ only as a man of excellent wisdom beyond all His peers. . . . But what mystery there lay in 'The Word was made flesh' I could not even imagine."[2]

II

How then are we to read this mystery for ourselves? Well, there *is* no reading of it, so long as we stand fast upon our human self-sufficiency, believing our conquests to be nothing but the fruit of our own free-will decisions, and our discoveries to be nothing but the fruit of our own perspicacity, and our upward progress to be nothing but the fruit of our own vitality and initiative. A view of life which leaves no room, behind and around and above our proud human achievements, for the gift of divine grace can never hope to find any meaning in the declaration that "God was in Christ." But if, on the contrary, we believe that the first and real initiative in all the forward movements of our spirits lies not with our finite wills but with the will of the Eternal God, if we believe that we could never love Him unless He first loved us, then the mystery begins to be a little more transparent to our minds.

The fundamental religious thought which

[1] *Confessions* vii, 9.   [2] *Ibid.* vii, 19.

we must here endeavour to grasp is that the
spiritual history of our race may, and indeed
must, be regarded from two different points of
view. On the one side of it, it is the history of
man's search for God—a long and arduous quest
on the part of the human heart, with much grop-
ing and much dark wandering and much missing
of the trail, to find Him who alone is heart's ease
and heart's desire. But on the other side of it, it
is the history, not of man seeking God, but of
God seeking man. Even within the narrow compass of our individual lives we have knowledge
of this "double search."[1] We know what our
pursuit of God is, with its defeats and its tri-
umphs, its hopes and its despairs; but we are
also conscious of that other and more unwearied
pursuit—the Hound of Heaven following after
us,

> ". . . with unhurrying chase,
> And unperturbed pace,
> Deliberate speed, majestic instancy."[2]

The outstanding fact of the spiritual life is not,
after all, that we seek the Good (for that we do
but brokenly and fitfully), but that the Good
seeks us and lays upon us its imperious claim;
and the primary data of the spiritual life are not
the little things we succeed in *doing*, but the

[1] The phrase is Dr. Rufus Jones's, whose little book, *The Double
Search: Studies in Atonement and Prayer* (Philadelphia, 1906),
deserves perpetuation as a minor classic of the spiritual life.

[2] Francis Thompson, *The Hound of Heaven.*

great things that we feel are being *required* of us by a Reality that far transcends our finite selfhood. And of the larger and longer story of humanity as a whole the same thing is true. It is not only a story of human faith, but also a story of divine grace. It is not only a story of human discovery, but also a story of divine revelation and self-disclosure. In short, it is a story, not merely of something achieved, but also of something received.

Yet there is one mistake we must be very careful not to make. We must not look at the matter as if *some* of our insights and our conquests were due purely to our own human initiative without any cooperation of the Divine Spirit at all, while *others* come to us purely as God's gift without any activity at all on the part of our own spirits. It is not true (as our fore-fathers persisted for many centuries in thinking) that we discover some things for ourselves, while other things are revealed to us by God. Rather are human discovery and divine revelation two complementary sides which we are bound to distinguish in every insight that we possess. God could never have revealed Himself to men who were not actively seeking to discover Him and, conversely, men could never have discovered a God who was not actively seeking to reveal Himself to them. Nor is it true that some passages in our human history are purely determined by our own free choices without any cooperation of the divine

will, while other passages are determined for us
entirely by God without our finite wills having
any say in the matter at all. The truth is rather
that human free-will and divine grace are two
complementary aspects of every forward movement of the human spirit; and this is a truth
which, if we are at present too much in reaction
against tradition to learn it from St. Augustine
or St. Thomas Aquinas or John Calvin, we can
learn almost equally well from any modern
philosopher who has grappled earnestly with the
problem of the freedom of the will. After all,
if there is no sense in which God can act through
and in the wills of men, then there is no sense
in which it is possible for Him to be active in
the human soul or in human life or in human
history. At most He could be regarded as having once long ago *started* human history—by de-
termining the evolution of our free-willed species from lower forms of life—and then leaving
it severely alone. Yet in a conception of that
kind there is no room at all for such a relationship between God and man as is worthy of the
name of religion.

Do we not here, then, reach at least the beginning of an understanding of that double significance which Jesus Christ has always had for
the life of the Christian fellowship? On the one
hand, He represents the highest point to which
our human race has yet attained. He stands, by
Himself alone, at the vanguard of our human

search for the Divine.[1] He is altogether one of
ourselves, a man among men, a human brother to
the lowliest among us, with the same handicaps
and the same opportunities. He had His human
chance just as you and I have ours; He had His
life to make or mar, and His human free-will
to make or mar it with. He differs from us only
in that He made more of His human opportunity than any of the rest of us has ever made
of ours, and used His free-will to better ends.
He is the great Discoverer, the great Trail-
finder, the great Leader of men and Himself
the Ideal Man to whose faith and patience and
bravery we must ever keep going back for guidance and inspiration until, as St. Paul says, we
all come unto the stature of His own fulness.[2]
But on the other hand we cannot read the story
of Christ's life without its being very strongly
borne in upon us that it marks the culmination,
not only of our human search for God, but also
of God's search for the human heart. This is a

[1] It may here be in place to remark that in no New Testament
writing is this double significance of the figure of our Lord more
clearly brought out than in the *Epistle to the Hebrews*, the teaching of which is thus summarised by Dr. Moffatt: ". . . the full
realisation of the fellowship with God which is the supreme object
of faith has now been made through Jesus. In two ways. (i) For
faith Jesus is the inspiring example; he is the great believer who
has shown in his own life on earth the possibilities of faith. . . .
But (ii) Jesus has not only preceded us in the line of faith; he
has by his sacrifice made our access to God direct and real, as it
never could be before." (*A Critical and Exegetical Commentary on
the Epistle to the Hebrews*, p. xliv.)

[2] *Ephesians* iv, 13.

story, we say, not only of great faith but of great
grace! This is a story not only of human discovery but of divine self-impartation! Here is
not only a Man raising Himself up towards
God, but God bending down to man! Here is
not only "one man's obedience" to God, but
God's generosity to all men! Moreover since it
is God's grace rather than our faith that is always the prior fact in the case (our free-will
being always undergirded by His indwelling
Spirit), so also we are bound to feel that this
Godward aspect of the evangelic history is really
prior to its manward aspect and of more vital
significance for the life of the Christian fellowship. The perfect manhood of Jesus is a *gift*
even more fundamentally than it is an achievement. The deepest sentiment to which it has
given rise in the minds of Christians throughout
all the ages is not pride and self-congratulation
at something our race has produced, but rather
gratitude at something it has received. We are
moved, all of us, not to applaud but to kneel;
not to clap our hands in admiration but to fold
them in worship.

III

It may, however, help us to a fuller realisation of the meaning of this Christian conviction
that "God was in Christ," if we remind ourselves
in some detail of the earlier ideas that men had

about the manner of the divine self-revelation. Ever since human history began, it had been believed that God had provided some means of making His will known to men. But at first men had the strangest ideas as to what these means were. They looked to what they called 'portents' and 'omens' appearing in the world of nature: they watched the flight of birds, they studied the markings in the entrails of sacrificial animals, they puzzled over the movements of the stars, in the hope that there might thus be revealed to them some sign or hint of the divine mind and will. A great advance was made when from this 'artificial divination,' as Cicero calls it, men passed to 'natural divination'—passed, that is, from the omen to the oracle, relying now, not on external signs, but on the plainly intelligible utterances of men and women who were supposed to be directly 'inspired' by God. Yet there unfortunately persisted in their conception of oracular inspiration one major fault which had attached itself to the old cult of the omen, namely the tendency to find God rather in abnormal and exceptional occurrences than in the ordinary course of things.[1] Men were held to be inspired by God, not when they were most wide-awake and at their human best, with their minds keen and their spirits eagerly seeking, but rather when

[1]"Put in simple language, it would seem to be urged that we could never believe God sent us our daily bread through bakers if He did not sometimes send it by a raven" (Lily Dougall, *God's Way with Man*, p. 39).

their normal personalities were wholly in abey-
ance, in sleep, in frenzy, in a swoon, or even in
some wholly psychopathic condition such as epi-
lepsy or madness. When the man's own mind
was clearly *not* behind the words coming out of
his mouth, then it was felt that God's mind
must be behind them. As time passed, however,
a few races began to leave behind them this second error also, and came to feel that God was
most clearly speaking to us, not when an ig-
norant and weak-minded maiden uttered gut-
tural sounds in a wild frenzy, but when the very
best and wisest men were speaking their very
best and wisest words. Nowhere did this development reach so pure a height as in the culminating period of Hebrew prophecy. The great
truth which there finds final recognition is that
God is to be looked for in the world nowhere
else than in *goodness* and that goodness is accordingly the only thing He requires of man.
The issue at stake is as to what things in our experience most clearly reveal to us the nature of
ultimate reality, and as to where we are to look
for the most reliable clue to the divine character,
the most unmistakable intimation of the divine
mind and will. And what the spiritual genius of
the Hebrew people now at last does is to point
us, not to any portentous occurrences in the realm
of the lower nature, nor yet to any words that
come from men's lips without seeming to come
from their minds, but rather to the highest

movements and achievements of the human
spirit itself (which are therefore not merely
achievements but also endowments)—love and
courage and honour and purity and truthfulness.
And I am sure there is not one of us who does
not know something of what this disclosure
means. Goodness, we all feel, is not a thing that
we build up for ourselves and out of ourselves
—"coral-reeflike," as Baron von Hügel used to
say,—it is a thing that beckons to us from beyond ourselves. Duty is not something we do
(for which of us ever satisfyingly does it?), it
is rather something we owe. And, as the poet
tells us,

> "The sense within me that I owe a debt
> Assures me—somewhere must be somebody
> Ready to take his due."

There is, however, one important respect in
which the Hebrew conception of revelation still
fails to satisfy the deepest divinings of our souls.
For there still persisted in the Hebrew mind
one relic and *damnosa hæreditas* of the old cult
of the oracle—namely the belief that God's way
of revealing His mind to men was to communicate to them certain verbal messages. The medium of the divine self-disclosure was believed
to be the spoken word, and accordingly, while
the prophets themselves were often very largely
forgotten, their inspired utterances were trea-
sured up in the national memory and were taken,

torn as they were from their natural context in the character and life of the prophet, to be the *ipsissima verba* of the Most High. The invention of writing brought to this mistake a further aggravation; for it came to be held by almost all literate peoples that the medium of revelation was not so much the spoken as the *written* word. God had revealed His will to men in *books;* and it was even held (as in Israel) that God Himself had written the original copy on tables of stone or (as in Islam) that He had dictated the sacred matter to the prophet from a parent copy, "the Mother of the Book," which existed above the stars. Yet I think we have all now come to feel that it is not in words and books that God reveals Himself, but in men; not in tables of stone but in the tables of the human heart. God is in words and books only because He is in the men behind the words and books. An inspired utterance only means the utterance of an inspired man. An inspired book only means a book written by a man in whom is the spirit of God. And instead of the book being better than the man, there is usually more in the man—in his living spirit, in his "little, nameless, unremembered acts"—than he is able to put into his book. Then there is a further insight which has come to us and which is very closely connected with this one. What is directly revealed to us, we feel, is not truths or doctrines about God, but God himself. Our doctrines about God are always secondary to our direct finding of God in the realities of our experience, and are never wholly adequate to that finding or wholly exhaustive of its meaning. God does not communicate with us: He does something far better—He communes with us. Not the communication of propositions but the communion of spirits is the last word about divine revelation.

IV

Now it is in the light of this long history that we are able to understand the real depth of significance that there is in the Christian finding of God in Christ. The Christian gospel is that the eternal Mind and Will have at last been fully revealed to us in a Man—the Man Christ Jesus. Here at last is the sign for which we mortals have been seeking ever since our history began! Through all the early ages we subjected the course of nature to the most pathetically painstaking of scrutinies. When we did not find Divinity in the marks on the bull's liver, we hoped we might find it in the patterns made by birds in their erratic flight; and when we did not find it there, we hoped we might still find it in the patterns which the stars made against the midnight sky! Then when that too failed us, we thought of the mysterious mutterings that men made in sleep or frenzy without knowing what they did, and we hoped it might turn out to be God who was speaking through them! All these false scents we followed, and many another, until at last wise men, like some of the Greeks, began to say that God had left us without any sign at all and that mortal man could never know what it was that really lay at the hidden heart of things. But now, in the fulness of the time, comes the "good news" of the Christian gospel! God has been revealed to us *in the soul of a man* —in that pure love that was the spirit of Jesus of Nazareth, in that simple tale of human goodness that was His life and in that poignant spectacle of human self-abnegation that was His death on the Cross. "To whom will ye liken God," a great Hebrew brooder had asked long centuries before, "or what likeness will ye compare unto Him?" And now at last we can answer and, pointing to that Life and that Death, can say, "Here is His likeness. He who hath seen this hath seen the Father." Now at last we know beyond assail of doubt where it is that the Eternal Oversoul descends into the familiar circuit of our poor human experience, and glorifies it with His most real presence, showing us Himself as He is and ourselves as we ought to be. There are uncounted centuries of most pathetic history behind the Pauline declaration that "God was in Christ,"[1] and behind the Johannine declaration that, though "no man hath seen God at

[1] *II Cor.* v, 19.

any time," yet ἐκεῖνος ἐξηγήσατο, "*He* hath made Him plain."[1]

There is still another point to be emphasised. If we are to understand all that the Christian Church has meant by the express presence of God in Christ, we must carefully avoid thinking or speaking as if God's revelation of Himself to man were a merely passive or otiose process on His part. The Christian gospel does not mean merely that God was always there to be found, and that now at last in Christ Jesus we have happened to succeed in finding Him. The Christian gospel is rather that in Christ God *did* something for the human race greater and more splendid than He had ever done before. Already, indeed, He had done enough to leave us, as St. Paul says, "without excuse,"[2] if we did not find Him at all. He had sent us Moses and the prophets (whom if we did not hear, neither should we have been persuaded if one had risen from the dead), He had sent us Socrates, He had sent us Gautama and Confucius and many more. And I do not see how we leave any room at all for God in our thoughts, or for the guidance of His Spirit in history, if we deny that, in some way and sense which we can only dimly understand, the advent of these leaders was part of His divine purpose and was definitely planned by Him with a view to the progress of mankind. Once again we must remember the farther side of the

[1] *John* i, 18.   [2] *Romans* i, 20.

Double Search and take its meaning seriously. After all, is it possible to regard any part of the upward movement of life on this planet of ours as purely an upthrusting from below? Must we not also think of it as being due to an attraction from above? The emergence of new forms, as Aristotle long ago pointed out, cannot possibly be explained unless we reckon not only with a *vis a tergo* but also with a *vis a fronte,* or (to substitute a modern biological terminology for that mediæval one) not only with a *poussée vitale* but also with an *attrait vital.* The attempt to explain any new emergent with reference only to its antecedents is nothing more or less than an attempt to get something out of nothing, and that is an attempt which no reasonable man would ever consciously make. But if this is true of the forward movement of life in general, it is doubly true of the forward movement revealed in the moral aspirations of the human species, because the primary datum of which we are here aware is not anything we have ourselves succeeded in achieving but rather a claim that is made upon us from beyond. If the 'is' cannot be explained in terms of mere creaturely will-power and *élan,* how much less can the 'ought' be so explained! We can thus have no difficulty of philosophical principle in understanding what religious faith has meant by the progressive self-revealing activity of God in our human history, but must rather be impelled to believe that in the advent of Jesus of Nazareth, and in His victory over sin, the Divine Father played no merely passive or permissive part, but actually *did* something for the enlightenment and salvation of our race. Undoubtedly it is this sense of the actual invasion of our human history by the gracious deed of God that accounts for the unparalleled joyfulness of the New Testament religion.

Yet we may still be asked what justification we can give for thus singling out one particular individual, Jesus of Nazareth, and finding in Him a special revelation of God. In our final chapter we shall be dealing at some length with certain aspects of this question, but meanwhile the general lines of our answer should be clear enough. There can surely be no difficulty in believing that the self-impartation of God in Christ was at least *as* 'special' as in our Christian experience it has actually proved itself to be. We must indeed be careful not to think or speak as if Jesus Christ were the only man in whom God has ever revealed Himself at all. Such an expungement of God's presence from all earlier and later history would come very queerly from the followers of One who to the end protested that He was come not to destroy but to fulfil. For it is this word 'fulfil' that answers our question. In the gospel history there is brought to fulfilment a divine invasion of our human life which is not totally absent from any history.

Twice in the New Testament it is affirmed that "No man hath seen God at any time"; yet it is very instructive to notice how differently the two verses are concluded. In the one case what is said is that though no man has ever seen God, yet whenever we see a man showing love to his brother, we see God there; while in the other case what is said is that though no man has ever seen God, yet when we see Jesus, we see God in Him.[1] But now these are not *two* findings of God, but only one. The Christian's finding of God in Christ is but the fulfilment of faith's older finding of Him in all love and goodness, wheresoever these are revealed to our human eyes. God is love. Where love is, there God is. And it is because men found in the soul of Jesus Christ the whole fulness of love, *and for no other reason*, that they found in Him the whole fulness of God.

We must indeed admit that there has often been a tendency among our theological pundits to interpret the incarnation of God in our Lord Jesus Christ as if it were a thing entirely by itself, an unrelated historical prodigy, for the understanding of which nothing else in our experience could give us any help or preparation at all. Yet surely to present the matter in this way is only to rob it of all its vitality of meaning, and to make men treat it once more as mere 'myth.' To believe in the interruption of ordinary his-

[1] *I John* iv, 12; *John* i, 18.

tory by the appearance of one prodigious and
miraculous event may indeed have a salutary
effect upon our dronish minds. It may rudely
shake up our complacent tendency to think that
there is nothing new under the sun and that the
humdrum of the common order of nature sets a
rigid limit to the creative omnipotence of the
Most High. But the advantage is bought at too
big a price, because we are at the same time encouraged to regard what we call 'ordinary' history as being, by contrast, even more ordinary
than before, and the 'common' order of nature
even more common than before, instead of rising to the higher (and alone truly liberating)
insight that there is no 'ordinary' history and no
'common' order of nature, because neither history nor nature is ever wholly uninvaded by
the express presence of that same God who was
manifest in Christ. It is good to be able to believe that the Omnipotent Love can intervene;
it is better still to be able to believe that He is
present all the time.

So with the author of the *Epistle to the Hebrews* we will say that the same "God who at
sundry times and in divers manners spake in
time past unto the fathers by the prophets, hath
in these last days spoken unto us by a Son . . ."[1]
Or with the equally unknown writer who, in the
next century, composed the *Epistle to Diognetus*
we will say that "This word of God was from

[1] *Hebrews* i, 1–2.

the beginning; it appeared anew, yet was proved
to be old; and it is always being born afresh in
the hearts of holy men."[1] Yet on the other
hand we must be equally careful not to allow
any shallow and lightly-adopted preconceptions
about the nature of historical progress to inter-
fere with our acknowledgement of the real
uniqueness and irreplaceableness of God's self-
revealing, self-imparting act in the advent of
our Lord. There is a tendency in our time to
speak of God's presence in Christ as being different only in *degree*, and not at all in *kind*,
from His presence in other men. But the distinction is after all an unreal one and is not without its perils. For surely the very glory and
headmark of all living history and living personality is just its uniqueness, its irreducible sin-
gularity and unrepeatability, its refusal to conform to any kind of quantitative computation of
measure or degree. So the question is not as to
the comparative measure of Christ's divinity, but
as to the particular and unique nature of the
work which, through and in Him, God has accomplished in our souls and in the world.[2] And
if it be really true that nowhere else are our human hearts touched as they are by the Gospel
story or our human need met as it is met by

[1] *Op. cit.*, xi, 4.

[2] *Cf.* O. C. Quick, *Liberalism, Modernism and Tradition*, p. 140,
and Baron F. von Hügel, *Essays and Addresses on the Philosophy
of Religion, Second Series*, p. 39.

Christ's redeeming love, then we shall soon find ourselves transcribing this blessed experience into the firm and confident belief that in this chapter of history God has been pleased to do something for our struggling humanity which He had never done before.

CHAPTER VII

SOME UNSATISFYING INTERPRETA-
TIONS

I

WE have now done our best to set forth, in terms suitable to our present-day comprehension, the meaning of the Christian conviction that God was in Christ. We have tried to do justice to that twofold significance which Christ has always seemed to have for His Church's life, as being not only its ideal of manhood but also its incarnation of Godhead. And I hope that in what has been said all the deep and characteristic values embedded in the older Christological tradition have been fully maintained and secured, however great and many the differences of external and theoretic form. It is impossible here to embark on any elaborate criticism of the older presentations, but we may profitably devote the present chapter to a brief examination of what may be regarded as the two most notable of the other ways in which men have sought to interpret the presence of God in Christ. If we can see clearly where these have been at fault, it will be of great aid to us in the building up of our own position.

Let us look first at the view which for many centuries seemed to hold the almost unbroken assent of Christendom—the view that our Lord Jesus Christ was a God-man who in His one 'person' combined the two 'natures' of man and God. This view was first officially adopted by the Church at the Fourth Ecumenical Council which met at Chalcedon in October 451. Before that date there had indeed been much discussion of the manner in which the 'divine nature' of God was united in the incarnation with the 'human nature' of Jesus of Nazareth, but in certain quarters there was a widespread tendency to hold that the two must have been united in such a way as to avoid any resultant duality of nature within Christ's person. It was this tendency which the Council of Chalcedon finally and authoritatively condemned, it being resolved that:

"This Council . . . anathematises those who imagine two natures of the Lord before the union, but fashion anew one nature after the union. Following, then, the holy fathers, we all with one voice teach that the Lord Jesus Christ is to us one and the same Son, the same perfect in deity, the same perfect in humanity; truly God and truly man; . . . of one essence with the Father in respect of His deity and of one essence with us in respect of His humanity; . . . to be acknowledged in two natures, without confusion, without mutation, without division, without separation; the distinction of two natures being in no way removed by the union, but rather the special character of each nature being preserved and concurring in one Person and one Substance . . ."[1]

All attempts to interpret the Figure of the Gospels as having a single 'nature' being thus ruled out as heretical, those who still found the alleged duality difficult to accept sought to find a way out of their perplexity by falling back on the weakened position that though Christ had two 'natures,' He had only one *will*. But in the year 680 the Sixth Ecumenical Council met at Constantinople and dealt with the doctrine of a single will in the same way as the earlier council had dealt with the doctrine of a single nature, affirming that within the single person of Christ there were not only two natures but also two wills. So 'Monothelitism' shared the same fate as 'Monophysitism.' And there the matter rested through all the Dark and Middle Ages, and through the period of Protestant orthodoxy, until with the awakening of the eager, critical modern mind it was once again involved in lively controversy.

Now we cannot be at all puzzled by the mention that is here made of a duality or twofoldness in reference to our Lord, because we have ourselves been all along insisting that He does indeed stand in a twofold relationship to the life of

---

[1] The Greek text of the Chalcedonian definition is conveniently given in T. H. Bindley's *The Œcumenical Documents of the Faith*.

the community He founded. But where we of to-
day cannot any longer follow the fathers who sat
at Chalcedon and Constantinople is in interpreting
this double significance which Jesus has for us
as implying a double nature which He has in
Himself. It is true that Jesus of Nazareth is one
of our human selves, and it is true that in Him
we nevertheless find the Eternal God plainly
revealed and present; yet we cannot think it to
follow from this that there must therefore have
been some kind of doubleness in what we might
call His mental make-up or psychical constitution, or that, as they said, in His single personality there coexisted, without division or separation yet also without confusion or permutation,
a nature as God and a nature as man. For it is
not as if we discovered His perfect humanity in
one side of His personality and one set of characteristics and of deeds, and His perfect divinity
in another side of His personality and another
set of characteristics and of deeds. It is not as if
sometimes the God in Him were manifest and
sometimes the man; nor is it as though when we
found least of man in Him then we found most
of God. We read as follows in the famous letter of Pope Leo I to Bishop Flavian of Constantinople, which was one of the documents adopted
as authoritative at Chalcedon:

"The lowliness of humanity and the loftiness of
divinity alternate with one another (*invicem sunt*).

For as the God is not changed by the pity, so the man is not absorbed by the dignity. For each nature does what is proper to itself in conjunction with the other—the Word performing what is proper to the Word and the flesh bringing to pass what is proper to the flesh. The one glitters with miracles, the other falls prey to injuries. . . . To be hungry, to be thirsty, to be weary and to sleep are evidently human. But to satisfy thousands of men with five loaves of bread and to bestow living water on the Samaritan woman, . . . and to walk on the surface of the sea . . . are undeniably divine."[1]

Yet to us this reasoning seems entirely perverse. We hardly know whether it is more wrong-headed to find in the hunger and thirst and weariness the characteristic marks of true humanity, or to find in the glittering miracles the characteristic marks of divinity. Hunger and thirst and weariness are the marks, not of our humanity, but of that brute nature that we share with the beasts, and unless we rose above these to higher spiritual potencies, we should not be worthy to be called *men* at all. The perfection of Christ's humanity was thus seen, not in the animal needs and weaknesses of His physical constitution, but in the upward and Godward striving of His spirit, above all in His perfect possession of that *faith* which He was always trying to awaken and develop in the minds of others. For indeed what could be more of the

[1] The text is in Bindley's *Œcumenical Documents*.

essence of our human situation, as finite spirits whose reach exceeds our grasp, who know the Infinite only in part and piecemeal, and see Him only as through a glass darkly, than just this attitude of faith? But now it is in this very faith that Jesus found the secret of His "glittering miracles," and it was on the conditioning faith rather than on the resulting wonders that His emphasis fell. "All things," He claimed, "are possible to him who has faith."[1] The physical miracles, indeed, were rather the least among faith's accomplishments than anything that went beyond its utmost powers. "Then came the disciples to Jesus apart, and said, Why could not we cast him out? And Jesus said unto them, Because of your unbelief: for verily I say unto you, If ye have faith as a grain of mustard seed, ye shall say unto this mountain, Remove hence to yonder place, and it shall remove; and nothing shall be impossible unto you."[2] And it is in this very faith, which was the crown and glory of Christ's humanity, and nowhere else, that we find the real presence of deity. For it was the constant teaching of Jesus that in all He did through faith, the real and ultimate doer was the Omnipotent God. To say that I can do a thing through faith in God is only a less significant way of saying that God can do that thing in and through me. To say that "all things are possible

[1] *Mark* ix, 23.
[2] *Matt.* xvii, 19–20; *cf. Luke* xvii, 6.

to him who has faith" is only a less significant
way of saying that "With men this is impossible;
but with God all things are possible."[1] So we see
that Leo, in the argument of his letter, was committing the very mistake against which we found
it necessary to warn ourselves in our last chapter. He was making faith and grace, discovery
and revelation, humanity and divinity refer to
different adjacent areas of our human experience, instead of recognising them to be two complementary aspects under which it is possible to
regard every forward and upward movement of
the human soul. He was attempting to unravel
from the one golden thread of our Lord's life
two distinct contiguous strands possessing what
he supposed to be the separate and opposite characteristics of God and of man. But as for ourselves, it is in the same characteristics and the
same graces of thought and will that we find
very man and very God; so that we shall say
with the poet, "Jesus, divinest when Thou most
art man!" In Him there is great faith, and what
is more human than faith? From Him there
streams great grace, and what is more divine
than grace? Yet it is in the faith, and nowhere
else, that we find the grace; and it is the grace,
and nothing else, that we believe to be the source
of the faith.

The Chalcedonian doctrine of the two natures
has recently been championed afresh by two able

[1] *Matt.* xix, 26; *cf. Mark* x, 27.

members of the Church of England—Canon O.
C. Quick and the Rev. J. K. Mozley,[1] but it has
been definitely abandoned by what is certainly
a majority of those who in our day have devoted independent reflection to this whole matter. And indeed it is difficult, in spite of all the
explanations of the two writers just mentioned,
to see what vital religious interest the doctrine
can be supposed to conserve. As marking a significant stage in the history of thought, the position defended by the fathers of Chalcedon
cannot fail to meet with the most sympathetic understanding on our part. When we realise that
what the Monophysite championship of a single
nature in Christ virtually amounted to, for the
mind of that time, was a denial of His real human nature and an attempt to conceive Him as
something not unlike a demigod (Monophysi-

[1]O. C. Quick, *Liberalism, Modernism and Tradition* (1922);
J. K. Mozley, "The Incarnation," in *Essays Catholic and Critical*,
ed. Selwyn (1926). "Starting from this fundamental conception
of Christ as Mediator," writes Canon Quick (p. 96), "Christian
theology was simply bound in the long run to think of Him in
one of two ways, either (i) as completely God and completely
man, or (ii) as some kind of being intermediate between God and
man, *i. e.*, a demigod or a superman." But these are just the two
conceptions which I am in this chapter concerned to criticise.
Mention should also be made of Bishop Gore's defence of Chalcedon in his *The Reconstruction of Belief*, pp. 513–524, and especially of his repudiation, in pp. 848–863, of Dr. Mackintosh's
criticism of Chalcedon (to which I refer below). It would have
been interesting to find Bishop Gore taking issue with the quite
similar criticism of Dr. Temple, now Archbishop of York (to
which I also refer). We may note also Mr. Lionel S. Thornton's
elaborate defence of the traditional view in *The Incarnate Lord*
(1928).

tism being to that extent always "Apollinarian" in tendency), then we realise that of the two positions we prefer that for which the Church decided. But that is not to say that either position can satisfy our present needs. The matter has been well argued by Prof. H. R. Mackintosh of Edinburgh in his well-known work on the subject. "For modern thought," he says, "the chief defect in strictly traditional Christology has been its insistence, not accidentally but on principle, upon what for brevity is called the doctrine of the two natures."

"Nicæa is a position gained once for all. Chalcedon, on the other hand, betrays a certain tendency, not merely to define, but to theorise. It embodies, even if faintly and as it were by allution, a particular form of interpretation which it is no real gain but a distinct loss to carry back in our minds to the study of the Gospels."

What has "invariably proved fatal to the doctrine of the two natures," he points out, has been the fact that, in spite of all attempts to find safe middle waters, it has always had to choose between being tossed on the Scylla of a duplex personality and the Charybdis of a denial of Christ's real manhood.

"If it takes Jesus' manhood seriously, as the New Testament of course does by instinct, it makes shipwreck on the notion of a double Self. If, on the other hand, it insists on the unity of the person, the unavoidable result is to abridge the integrity of the manhood and present a Figure whom it is difficult to identify with the Jesus of the Synoptic Gospels."[1]

Another and earlier Scottish statement will be found in Prof. D. W. Forrest's *The Christ of History and Experience*, which was published in 1897, and in which it is most clearly perceived that if in the Person of our Lord the divine and human natures remained to the end distinct, then there was after all no real incarnation of divinity in humanity. The Chalcedonian definition, he writes,

"conveys too abstract a conception of Christ's Deity *as it existed in the Incarnation,* by bringing together the two natures in their totality, as if the divine attributes remained in all respects unchanged. But this is to be untrue to the actual revelation which it professes to interpret. . . . The Gospels show that, however wide and deep His knowledge, . . . yet it was not omniscient. Still more plainly, He was not omnipresent. . . . Nor did He retain His omnipotence. . . . So long as these facts were not perceived or faced, it was natural that the Church, notwithstanding the Creed of Chalcedon, should remain, as it did for centuries, practically monophysite. The human consciousness of Christ was phantasmal."[2]

And we may call also to our support the Archbishop of York:

[1] *The Doctrine of the Person of Jesus Christ* (1912), pp. 292–297.
[2] *Op. cit.*, pp. 194 f.

"The formula of Chalcedon is, in fact, a confession of the bankruptcy of Greek patristic theology."[1]

Where then lay the explanation of this very serious error? It lay undoubtedly in the stubborn tradition, coming entirely from Greek sources, which made human nature a thing quite different in kind from the nature of God. The ultimate background of the tendency is doubtless to be found in the popular religion of ancient Greece, but it was Aristotle who first encouraged its elevation into a philosophical doctrine. His teaching was that the universe consists essentially of two layers, one of which reaches up to just below the moon and may be called the sublunary world, while the other extends from the sphere of the moon to the outermost sphere of the fixed stars and may be called the celestial world. To these two halves of the universe he attributes fundamentally different and even opposite properties. Below the moon everything moves in a straight line, while above the moon everything moves in a circle. Terrestrial bodies are made of the four elements of earth, water, air and fire, but celestial bodies have a totally different constitution, consisting entirely of a fifth element ($\pi \acute{\epsilon} \mu \pi \tau o \nu$ $\sigma \hat{\omega} \mu \alpha$, whence our word *quintessence*) called ether. And by this dualism Aristotle's outlook was largely determined. "The very scanty knowl-

[1]*Foundations*, ed. Streeter, p. 230.

edge," we find him beautifully interjecting in one of his writings on natural history, "which we can attain of celestial beings is sweeter to us by reason of its excellence than all our knowledge of the world in which we live, just as it is sweeter to get the tiniest and most casual glimpse of those we love than to get a detailed view of all other things, however many and great."[1] The disastrous effect which this departure from the earlier position of Plato continued to exercise in the realm of physical science right down to the time of Galileo is now a familiar enough topic of the historians, but its baneful effects on the course of religious dogma have been less often recognized.

Yet a further trouble was introduced by the use of the word 'nature' ($\phi\acute{\upsilon}\sigma\iota\varsigma$). This is a word whose original associations were entirely with physical science and which has properly no business at all in the discussion of matters spiritual. In this case the responsible persons are the Stoics, who were the first to give the word an ethical and psychological application, speaking of 'human nature' and of the 'nature' of God. They had a right, of course, to use the word as they chose, but the mischief lay in the fact that there still clung to their employment of it more than a few of its old associations with the realm of matter. The Stoics were, from first to last, most crudely materialistic in their conception of

[1] De Part. An., i, 5.

spirit, and always regarded it as being only a highly rarefied kind of matter, like a flame.

In the semi-popular philosophical eclecticism of the early Christian centuries these two traditions seem to have joined hands. Humanity seems to have been understood by all to be a kind of soul-substance which human beings possess as a substratum beneath the phenomena of their mental life; and divinity was taken to be a soul-substance similarly possessed by God; and the two were thought of as essentially *different* substances. We now believe this view to have been mistaken. God's nature and man's nature, we believe, are not different in *kind*, because in kind they are both *spiritual* nature, both *ethical* nature. We are men and are above the brutes—we have human and not merely animal nature—because God has breathed into us the breath of *His own* spiritual life. God's nature is, in the wholeness of eternal and infinite perfection, that to which our human nature gropingly and blunderingly, and ever imperfectly, strives to attain. God's nature is love, and man's nature is trying to be love. Indeed that, for us, is the very meaning of the Incarnation—that it is in Christ's very humanity, and not in some other nature which He had alongside of His humanity (however closely united with it), that God is to be found. The Christian announcement is not that there once appeared in our world a prodigious being with two natures—two natures "in essence so disparate, so utterly unrelated and heterogeneous, that a miracle of sheer omnipotence is needed to unite them."[1] The Christian announcement is, quite centrally and essentially, that *God* was made manifest to us in a *Man*—in a soul of like passions with our own but controlled to finer ends, in a life of simple faith and quiet helpfulness lived out under human conditions in its own little niche of time and place, and in a cruel death bravely borne.

II

The other false alternative which I wish to contrast with the position developed in the foregoing chapter is the type of view known as adoptianism.[2] This may be very simply described as the tendency to regard Jesus Christ, not as God become man, but as a man who became divine. The divine significance of our Lord is thus explained, not in terms of incarnation, but in terms of deification or—to use the Greek word—of apotheosis.

The adoptianist tendency in Christology seems to have been in competition with the more generally accepted Incarnation view from a very early period in the history of dogma, and in the later days when the Incarnation view was

[1]H. R. Mackintosh, *op. cit.*, p. 214.
[2]Sometimes also written 'adoptionism' by English writers.

officially interpreted in the sense of the doctrine of the two natures, adoptianism represents at least one of the several strands of tendency that went to make up the Arian, Monophysite and Monothelite oppositions. Some writers[1] find an inchoate adoptianist Christology in the thought of the Synoptic evangelists; many more writers find it in the speeches attributed to St. Peter in the early chapters of the *Acts of the Apostles*[2]; but into this obscure region of controversy we need not here enter. Militant adoptianism is first found in formal conflict with the official view in the teaching of one Theodotus, a Constantinopolitan who taught in Rome and was excommunicated by Pope Victor in the last decade of the second century. But it has been argued by Harnack that all through the apostolic and sub-apostolic ages an outlook of substantially the same type had been prevalent in the minds of many Gentile Christians especially in the *Vulgärchristentum* of the simple uneducated people. The outstanding example of such an outlook is in the writing known as *The Shepherd of Hermas*, dating most probably from the early years of the second century. The two facts that this is a Roman writing and that before the end of the century adoptianism was so outspokenly present in Rome in the group of which Theodotus was the

[1] *E. g.*, Dean Inge, *Outspoken Essays, Second Series*, p. 41.
[2] *E. g.*, *Acts* ii, 32–36; v, 30–31.

leader, have led Prof. Kirsopp Lake to suggest
that the Christianity of the Church at Rome
was from a very early time quite generally
adoptianist in character, the alternative Incarna-
tion-Christology being in an equally definite
manner connected with the Church at Ephesus.[1]
However this may be, there seems little doubt
that we have here to do with a tendency of
thought which, in one form or another, repeat-
edly manifested itself in the attempts of the
free-lance thinkers of a slightly later period to
find escape from the difficult corner into which
they felt they were gradually being shepherded
by the official definitions of the faith.

Speaking very generally, what was held was
that Jesus was a man who as the result of perfect conformity to the will of God became divine or (as it is otherwise put) to whom deity
was communicated as the reward of such conformity. He is thus said to be the 'adopted'
Son of God—and hence the name 'adoptian,' to
have been 'raised' to divinity, to have 'earned
the name' of God or of Lord. There is no clear
agreement as to whether the elevation in question was a gradual or a sudden one or, if the
latter, as to the point in His career at which it
took place. The view of Theodotus and his
group of followers was that the Virgin Birth
of Christ was already, in the foreknowledge of

[1]See K. Lake, *The Stewardship of Faith*, Ch. vii; *Landmarks in
the History of Early Christianity*, Ch. v.

God, a kind of anticipative conferring of divine honour; that after His perfect holiness and obedience had been tested for thirty years and not found wanting, special divine powers were conferred upon Him through the Holy Spirit on the occasion of His Baptism; and that finally, at His Ascension, He was 'adopted' into the sphere of divinity. Two generations later we find practically the same view reappearing in Paul of Samosata who, because he held it, was deposed from his bishopric of Antioch in Syria by a synod which met there in 269. Another half-century goes by and we find the same idea present, though here mingled with certain other strains of thought, in the teaching of Arius[1] and his followers, so that one of the battle-cries used against them by their Athanasian opponents was that Christ was divine *"natura, non adoptione."* And so at intervals the tendency kept persistently rearing its head, even to the age of Charlemagne, when the outspoken adoptianism (now first proudly owning to the name) of two Spanish bishops, Elipandus of Toledo and Felix of Urgel, was condemned by synods meeting at Ratisbon and Aix-la-Chapelle. It was only with the coming of the Scholastic period that all opposition to the orthodox view seemed at last to disappear.

But in our modern day, when the difficulty of

[1] The connection of Arius with Paul of Samosata was through Arius' teacher, Lucian of Antioch.

accepting the idea of incarnation in its official form of the two-nature theory has once again become acute, there has been a tendency in not a few quarters to revert to something very like adoptianism. It is indeed adoptianism with a difference, adoptianism readjusted to suit our modern ideas of progress and evolution, but it represents what is fundamentally the same attempt at escape. With the freshly-unveiled picture of the historical Jesus before us, it has sometimes seemed to us easier to find some way of calling Him a 'Divine Man,' and to think of Him as One who had earned the title of divinity, than to regard Him as God become man and retaining both natures in one person. We have, as Canon Quick very truly remarks, sometimes "tortured" our "brains in order to find means to predicate Deity of a mere man, with the inevitable result that Deity becomes a mere predicate."[1]

Yet there is here no real way out of our difficulty. It is after all only on the surface that adoptianism seems easier than the 'two natures.' To say that Jesus of Nazareth became divine is in a sense to say far too much and in a sense to say far too little. It is to say too much, because, as Prof. Lake rightly insists, "We cannot believe that at any time a human being, in consequence of his virtue, became God, which he was not before, or that any human being will

[1] *Op. cit.*, p. 50.

ever do so."[1] It is to say too much, because, as another writer warns us, it would involve us in what can only be described as "the idolatrous deification of a Jew."[2] A deified man is, in fact, only one degree less mythical than two natures in one person. But it is also to say far too little, because the real essence of the Christian gospel is not that one Man has raised Himself up to God but rather that God has come down through one Man into our whole human life. It is no deified man that can help us but only God Himself——

> "God's presence, and His very self
> And essence all-divine."

I think we can see, then, that in the end both the false alternatives of which I have here spoken—adoptianism and the theory of the two natures—are rendered impossible of our acceptance because they share the same fault. They both ten.[1] to state the Christian confession as if it centred in a conviction concerning the nature of Jesus of Nazareth.[3] But what we have now

[1] *Landmarks in the History of Early Christianity*, p. 101.

[2] A. E. J. Rawlinson, *The New Testament Doctrine of the Christ*, p. 227.

[3] I am grateful for Canon Quick's statement that the doctrine of the two natures "had no primary reference to the psychological problem of the consciousness of the God-man in the days of His flesh" (*op. cit.*, p. 95). Here are two other recent pronouncements to the same general effect: "It is on the ground of what He achieved historically that Paul identified Jesus with the Son of

come to feel so strongly is that the real centre and burden of the Christian confession is a conviction concerning the nature of God. "He that believeth on me," says the Christ of the Fourth Gospel, "believeth not on me, but on him that sent me."[1] "He appeared at the end of the ages," we read of Christ in *First Peter*, "for the sake of you who through him believe in God, who raised him from the dead and gave him glory, so that your faith and hope might be in God."[2] There is perhaps no point which has been more insisted on by recent writers than this. Here is Dr. Temple, now Archbishop of York:

"The central doctrine of Christianity has been made unduly difficult by the way in which believers inevitably tend to state it. It is really a doctrine about God; but it is made to appear as if it were primarily a doctrine about a historic Person, who lived at the beginning of our era. . . . To ask whether Christ is Divine is to suggest that Christ is an enigma while Deity is a simple and familiar conception. But the truth is

God who is the 'life-giving Spirit' of humanity. This, it may be suggested, is a firmer ground for the building of a 'Christology' than minute psychological analysis of the meagre data concerning the self-consciousness of Jesus in the Gospels" (Prof. C. H. Dodd, *The Meaning of Paul for To-day*, pp. 89 f.). "It is idle to disguise the fact that this whole subject of Jesus' conception of His person is shrouded in obscurity and uncertainty. The influence of the dogmatic faith of the Church in shaping the tradition is patent to every candid student, and how much will be left standing after a sane criticism has done its work, it is hard to say" (Prof. Wm. Morgan, *The Nature and Right of Religion*, p. 228).

[1] *John* xii, 44.
[2] *I Peter* i, 20–21.

the exact opposite to this. . . . The wise question is not, 'Is Christ Divine?' but, 'What is God like?' "[1]

And again more recently:

"Remember that the importance of all we say about Him comes from the consequent thought of God. . . . God is Christlike. The majesty which rules all things is the majesty of such love as we see in Christ."[2]

Here is Principal Cairns of Aberdeen:

"The Christian confession of Jesus as Son of God is not only a confession about Christ. It is an affirmation about the Universe. It is an affirmation of faith that it is Christ's world, of belief in the Christlikeness of Almighty God."[3]

And here is Dean Inge of St. Paul's:

"The controversy about the Divinity of Christ has in fact been habitually conducted on wrong lines. We assume that we know what the attributes of God are, and we collect them from any sources rather than from the revelation of God in Christ. We maintain that, in spite of His voluntary humiliation, Christ possessed all the attributes of the unlimited Sultan of the universe before whom other creeds are willing to do homage. But surely Christ came to earth to reveal to us, not that He was like God, but that God was like Himself."[4]

And what three sounder thinkers are there among us than these?

[1] In *Foundations* (ed. Streeter), pp. 213 f., 259.
[2] In an article on "How can we find God?" in *The Christian Century* (Chicago) for 28th February, 1929.
[3] *The Army and Religion*, p. 284.
[4] *Outspoken Essays, Second Series*, p. 49.

III

In our own time it is not uncommon to find the more nervous defenders of tradition putting to their fellow men, as a test of their essential Christianity, the apparently plain and pointed question, "Do you believe that Jesus was God?" To this question a great many of our contemporaries are obliged to answer 'No,' not because they feel themselves out of sympathy with the Christian gospel, but because their minds grow dark before the notion that the Man of Nazareth was simply *identical* with the Eternal Spirit in whom we all live and move and have our being. Yet there is here no need at all for any one to distress himself; for the statement that "Jesus is God," taken thus by itself, is not orthodox, let alone true. It is an extreme product of uninstructed modern controversy, which Athanasius himself would not have accepted in the sense which is nowadays given to it. Something like it may perhaps be found in Luther, or in the later Lutheran teaching concerning the so-called *communicatio idiomatum*, so uniformly rejected by the Zwinglians and Calvinists "as leading to the deification of our Lord's manhood"[1]; but to Catholic orthodoxy this is still the "Lutheran heresy." And in fact, if the truth about the presence of God in Christ were as

[1] H. R. Mackintosh, *op. cit.*, p. 243. See also F. Loofs, *Leitfaden zum Studium der Dogmengeschichte*, 3 Aufl., § 81, 7 and § 87, 7.

severely simple and elementary as the dictum "Jesus was God" would make it seem, it would hardly have taken so many centuries of Christo-logical dogma to beat it out. I take it that the fathers of Nicæa and Chalcedon were at least as eagerly concerned to uphold the very human-ity of Christ as to uphold the presence in Him of very God, and that they would have pro-nounced the bare statement that Jesus was God to have been as far from adequate to the whole truth they were desirous of expressing as the bare statement that He was man.[1] That is why

---

[1] There was a most instructive private correspondence on this very point between the late Principal Denney of Glasgow and the late Sir William Robertson Nicoll in the December of 1908. The correspondence can be put together from *Letters of Principal James Denney to W. Robertson Nicoll 1893–1917*, pp. 120–126 and T. H. Darlow's *William Robertson Nicoll, Life and Letters*, pp. 360–365. A brief abstract of it may here be made. The occasion was the appearance of Denney's notable book on *Jesus and the Gospel*, and the correspondence begins with Nicoll writing to Denney on Dec. 4th: "I kept on reading in search of an unequivo-cal statement that Jesus is God. Very likely I have missed it, but I did not find it." On Dec. 7th Denney replies: "As for your remark that you missed an unequivocal statement that Jesus is God, I feel inclined to say that such a statement seems unattrac-tive to me just because it is impossible to make it unequivocal. It is not the true way to say a true thing. . . . I dread ways of putting it [the Catholic doctrine of the Trinity] which do nothing but challenge contradiction. 'Jesus is God' seems to me one of these provocative ways, and therefore I avoid it. It has the same objectionableness in my mind as calling Mary the mother of God. The N. T. says θεὸς ἦν ὁ λόγος, but it does not say ὁ λόγος ἦν ὁ θεός, and it is this last which is really suggested to the English mind by 'Jesus is God.' Last week the Rev. Dawson Walker . . . sent me a penny book on the Trinity he has written, . . . He takes this, as I think, mistaken line: 'Jesus Himself claimed to be God,' etc. I can only say that the wrong things it suggests seem to me so completely to outbalance the right that we can well afford to dispense with it." The next day Nicoll wrote

they condemned the Docetists who taught that in reality Jesus was God *simpliciter* and only *appeared* to be a man, and the Apollinarians who taught that His mind was the mind of God *simpliciter* and only His body was human.

The fact is that such a formula as "Jesus is

back, "For my part I should still think it correct to say that Jesus claimed to be God and that He was God. . . . I can see that there is much room for discussion of the Person of Christ, but I do from my heart believe that God was manifest in the flesh." Three days later Nicoll wrote a perplexed letter on the matter to Prof. H. R. Mackintosh, in which he says of Denney, "There is a singular vein of scepticism in him, for all his apparent orthodoxy." Denney's final reply, written on Dec. 12th, includes the following: "I really do not think there is any difference between us. When you say that you do from your heart believe that God was manifest in the flesh, I am sure I can say the same. . . . Probably the aversion I have to such an expression as Jesus is God is linguistic as much as theological. We are so thoroughly monotheistic now that the word God, to put it pedantically, has ceased to be an appellative and become a proper noun: it *identifies* the being to whom it is applied so that it can be used as the subject of a sentence; but it does not unfold the nature of that being so that it could be used as the predicate in a sentence. In Greek, and in the first century, it was quite different. You could say then ὁ Ἰησοῦς θεός ἐστιν. But the English equivalent of that is not Jesus is God (with a capital G), but, I say it as a believer in His true deity, Jesus is god (with a small g—not *a* god, but a being in whom is the nature which belongs to the one God). I have no objection at all to Parker's formula, Jesus is God the Son, because 'the Son' introduces the very qualification of God which makes it possible to apply it to Jesus. In the same way I have no hesitation in saying Jesus was God *manifest in the flesh*, because 'manifest in the flesh' serves the same purpose. It is because God is to all intents a proper noun with us, which, if it is used as a predicate at all, must make an equation with the subject (Jesus is God being the same thing as Jesus=God), that it seems not only to me, but I am sure to most people, an unnatural way of declaring their faith in Christ as Immanuel—God with us. Jesus is man as well as God, in some way therefore both less and more than God; and consequently a form of proposition which in our idiom suggests inevitably the precise equivalence of Jesus and God does some kind of injustice to the truth."

God," if indeed it says too much for our comprehension, says also too little for our salvation. In committing ourselves to the doctrine of our Lord's divinity we are committing ourselves, not to some quaint legend of a bygone age, nor yet to any bewildering dogma of scholastic fashioning, but to something infinitely more exacting and more testing. We are committing ourselves to the declaration that the things which Jesus stood for are the most real things, the things that matter most, in all the world. We are committing ourselves to the declaration that love and not justice, love and not force, forgiveness and not requital, giving and not getting, compassion and not aloofness, self-spending and not self-saving, are the pillars on which the universe is built. We are embracing the faith that love, in howsoever humble guise appearing, in whatsoever weakness manifesting itself, is omnipotent, and that Omnipotence is love. In truth, there is hardly anything at all of the Christian gospel in the bare announcement that to the person of Jesus of Nazareth we can attach the old fixed predicate of deity, as if we were saying merely that He were Jupiter or Yahweh or the World-soul of the Stoic schools. The Christian gospel is rather that we must radically revise our old conception of deity in the light of the new predicate of Christlikeness. And it was this gospel that conquered the Roman Empire. The Romans of that age were fond enough of deifying people. They found no difficulty at all in calling men God. Christianity had nothing new to tell them there. But what kind of man was it whom they deified? It was Julius Cæsar with his dazzling royalty and his hard justice and his lust for power. It was Tiberius and Claudius with their privileged and suspicious weakness. It was Caligula and Nero with their brutality and pomp and greed. That, apparently, was what the Romans had come to think that God was like! And then there came to them a little band of men from the Eastern provinces who, when they were asked what God was like, told a strangely contrasted story of a humble Jewish artisan who, while these kings of the Gentiles were exercising lordship, had been among men as he that serveth; who all His life had gone about doing good and healing all who were oppressed of the devil; who had spent His time not with the righteous but with sinners; who when He was reviled, reviled not again; and who at the last chose even to die that others might live. And do you remember Matthew Arnold's dramatic description of the result?

"She heard it, the victorious West,
　In crown and sword array'd!
She felt the void which mined her breast,
　She shiver'd and obey'd.

She veil'd her eagles, snapp'd her sword,
　And laid her sceptre down;

Her stately purple she abhorr'd
  And her imperial crown.

She broke her flutes, she stopp'd her sports,
  Her artists could not please;
She tore her books, she shut her courts,
  She fled her palaces;

Lust of the eye and pride of life
  She left it all behind,
And hurried, torn with inward strife,
  The wilderness to find.

Tears wash'd the trouble from her face!
  She chang'd into a child!
'Mid weeds and wrecks she stood—a place
  Of ruin—but she smiled!"

CHAPTER VIII

ATONEMENT

I

THE Christian's thought of his Lord Jesus Christ has from the beginning seemed to revolve round two focal ideas —the idea of incarnation and the idea of atonement. In the last two chapters we have dealt fully with the former of these ideas. Now we must devote a chapter to the latter. Nowhere, indeed, does the double-sidedness of our modern feeling towards the traditional Christological scheme receive more notable illustration than in the case of this doctrine. On the one hand, we seem to find in the old presentation nothing but a bristling mass of difficulties; yet on the other hand, when we try to put the matter in our own modern way, we nearly always find that we have left out some vital element of religious truth or some quite essential religious appeal which the old presentation successfully included. The problem of how to sift out all the grains of baser metal without losing any of the pure gold appears here in its very acutest form.

It is true that our situation with regard to
the doctrine of atonement is not quite the same
as was our situation with regard to the doctrine
of incarnation, inasmuch as the former was
never given that rigid authoritative definition
which the latter received at the councils of
Nicæa, Chalcedon and Constantinople. It may
rightly be said, therefore, that there is no
'orthodox' doctrine of atonement. Indeed the
type of doctrine of atonement which prevailed
in the Western Church throughout the centuries when the doctrine of incarnation was being given its final definition by the councils is
one whose characteristic features came, during
the Middle Ages, to be definitely repudiated
by all the Church's most responsible spokesmen,
so that it is not now necessary to argue against
it. This was what is known as the 'ransom theory,' its interpretation of the Christian redemption being that the death and three-days' descent into hell of Jesus Christ the Son of God
was a ransom paid to the devil for the release
from hell of mankind which, through the sin
of Adam, had become his inalienable property.
Though never worked out by any thinker in a
thorough-going and systematic way, this ex-
traordinary conception held the almost unchal-
lenged assent of Christendom for a thousand
years, until at the end of the eleventh century
certain features of it were valiantly attacked by

Anselm, the saintly Italian who became famous as Archbishop of Canterbury under William Rufus and Henry the First of England. Anselm's book, *Cur Deus Homo*, is really the first fully thought-out statement of the doctrine of the atonement in Christian literature. Yet though it stands for a quite epoch-making improvement, the extent of its disagreement with the older view of the matter must not be overestimated. For the thought of Christ's death as the payment of a ransom to the devil, Anselm substituted the thought of it as the payment of a debt to God; but the lapse of another eight centuries has made this change, vitally significant as it undoubtedly was, seem almost a small thing in comparison with the large area of doctrine which the two theories held in common. For our purposes, therefore, and in spite of certain features of his view which were afterwards modified by the Schoolmen of the thirteenth century or by the Protestant Reformers, Anselm's statement may be taken to represent the strictly traditional doctrine of atonement at its best and clearest. What I propose to do in this chapter is first to offer a brief summary of Anselm's theory, then to indicate the respects in which we nowadays feel ourselves to be out of sympathy with it, and finally to set forth the permanent elements of truth which I believe it to contain.

could do so, if the logic of justice permitted Him; for supposing God should offer to suffer death for our sakes, then indeed that death "would outweigh all the sins of mankind."[1] The required satisfaction is thus one "which only God can, and only man should, make."[2] The only possibility of escape is therefore that "a God-man should be found,"[3] that is to say, "one who is both God and man," and is able to do it as God, while being permitted to do it as man.

"For God will not do it because He ought not, and man will not do it because he cannot; therefore in order that God-and-man (*deus homo*) may do this, it is necessary that he who is to make this satisfaction should in his same person be perfect God and perfect man; for he cannot do it unless he be very God, nor ought unless he be very man."[4]

This way out God, in His great mercy, has chosen. He caused the second Person of His divine Trinity to be united with the manhood of Adam's race and so to appear among us as a

[1]Book II, Ch. XIV.　　　[2]Book II, Ch. VI.
[3]Book II, Ch. VII: "necesse est inveniri deum hominem."
[4]Book II, Ch. VII. *Cf.* Calvin: "Finally, since as God only He could not suffer, and as man only could not overcome death, He united the human nature with the divine, that He might subject the weakness of the one to death as an expiation of sin, and by the power of the other, maintaining a struggle with death, might gain us the victory" (*Institutio*, Book II, Ch. XII, § 3; Henry Beveridge's translation).

God-man and suffer death for our salvation. Jesus of Nazareth was this God-man, and His death on the cross was this death.

Such, in briefest outline, is Anselm's account of the Christian redemption.

III

In trying now to single out the numerous 'snags' which such a scheme contains for our minds and hearts and consciences to-day, I shall not concern myself at all with such difficulties as are purely intellectual in character—like those connected with the pre-Copernican cosmological framework in which Anselm's whole theory is set or with his pre-evolutionary conception of the descent of our race from a single human pair. Such difficulties, after all, are comparatively easy to smooth out. The difficulties I shall mention are all of an ethical and religious nature.

First, and casting its sinister shadow over everything else, there is Anselm's view of God as being in His most ultimate nature, not a loving father, but a monarch and taskmaster, whose first concern is for His own dignity and prestige, though these are not presented as bearing any necessary relation to the proper good of His creatures. This is the same as to say that justice rather than love is the fundamental prin-

ciple of the spiritual universe.[1] *Second,* there is
the fact, following from this, that when the
love of God *is* introduced, it appears as a
secondary element in His nature, which is in
conflict with His justice or desire for honour.
Third, there is the tendency which is subtly
present throughout, and which is no doubt
closely bound up with the two points already
mentioned, to make one's own salvation, rather
than the service of one's fellows, the object of
first importance for our thoughts.[2] *Fourth,*
there is the tendency to be more troubled about
the future punishment of sin than about the
present estrangement from God which it en-
tails. *Fifth,* there is the whole conception of
punishment as inflicted by God in retributive
anger and in spite of His love for us, as against
the higher conception that "whom the Lord
loveth he chasteneth" and that, if we are pun-
ished, it is because God dealeth with us "as with

[1]Yet, as Dean Rashdall rightly says, "A God who really thought
that His honour was increased by millions of men suffering eternal
torments, or that it was a satisfactory compensation to Himself
that in lieu thereof an innocent God-man should suffer upon the
cross, would not be the God whom Anselm in his heart of hearts
really worshipped" (*The Idea of Atonement in Christian Theology,*
p. 356).

[2]"Nevertheless," as Canon Streeter truly says, reminding us
that the practical religion of the Church constantly rose above
these errors of its formal theology, "the gates of Hell could not
prevail entirely against the call to adventure which rings out in
the words and acts of Christ. The cathedral-builders, the knight-
errant, St. Francis, soared above that ethic of 'safety first' which
is the legal corollary of a religion based on fear [of Hell]" (*Adventure,* p. 54).

sons." *Sixth*, there is the discrepancy (which remains in spite of all that may and must be said
about the solidarity of the race and the known
facts of heredity) between Anselm's idea that
God imputes the guilt of the first man's trans-
gressions to every one of his descendants and
our own known duty not to punish children for
the sins of their fathers. "Anselm," writes the
late Dean Rashdall, "appeals to justice, and
that in all good faith; but his notions of justice
are the barbaric ideas of an ancient Lombard
king or the technicalities of a Lombard lawyer
rather than the ideas which would have satisfied such a man as Anselm in ordinary human
life. . . . No civilized system of law permits
the attribution of guilt to all humanity for the
sin of one."[1] *Seventh*, there is the difficulty that
the saving love of God is allowed to be operative towards man only in the one act of His
sending Jesus Christ to us.[2] *Eighth*, there is the
difficulty that even in that one case it is allowed

[1] *Op. cit.*, p. 355.

[2] This is expressly admitted. At the end of Book I (in Chapter
XXIV) we read, "If God follows the logic of justice, there is no
way by which our unfortunate race can escape, and God's mercy
seems to vanish. . . . I do not deny the mercy of God who saves
man and beast 'according to the multitude of His mercy.' But
we are speaking about that final mercy which makes man blessed
after this life." Then at the end of Book II (in Chapter XX) we
read, "So the mercy of God which, when we were considering
God's justice and man's sin, seemed to you to vanish, we find
now to be so great and at the same time so congruous with justice that neither greater nor juster can be imagined." And it is
made plain that this changed judgement is in consideration of
God's offering up of His Son on Calvary, and of nothing else.

to be operative only by means of a legal artifice —an act of substitution of one for many and of guiltless for guilty which, however beautiful it may be when regarded as an act of love, cannot be held to satisfy the demands of strict justice in the sense necessary for Anselm's theory. "It fails completely," says Principal Oman of this substitutionary theory in general, "to fulfil the legal conditions of the very legal difficulty it exists to remove."[1] *Ninth,* there is the difficulty that this legal artifice is closely bound up with that conception of Jesus of Nazareth as having in His single person "two natures," which we have already found to be so inadequate to faith's true view of Him. *Tenth,* there is the fact that what is here held to be effective for our redemption is not what direct experience proclaims it to be, namely the spirit in which Jesus faced His death, but is rather the mere fact that He was slain.[2] *Eleventh,* there is the fact, as troublesome to our minds as any I have mentioned, that the way by which the love of God is here allowed to be effective for the forgiveness of wrongs committed against

[1]*Grace and Personality*, 2nd ed., p. 206. *Cf.* Rashdall: "Nor can the payment of a penalty by the sinless Christ rationally or morally be considered to make any easier or any juster the remission of the penalty which man owes for his sin" (*op. cit.*, p. 355).

[2]Yet Anselm finely insists that Christ went ito His death of His own free will. "God did not compel Christ to die; but Christ suffered death of His own free will, not from any obligation to give up His life, but on account of the obligation He was under to fulfil all righteousness, in which He so firmly persevered that He incurred death thereby" (Book I, Ch. IX).

Him seems to bear no relation to the way in which our human love is often effective for the forgiveness of wrongs committed against ourselves. The air of unreality, and of remoteness from direct spiritual experience, which is thus given to Anselm's theory would have been avoided, had he brought his mind to bear more fixedly on the saying, "Forgive us our debts, as we forgive our debtors."

IV

Now let us turn to the more welcome, if also more delicate and difficult, task of trying to set forth the real and unchanging elements of truth that lie behind this whole conception of atonement with God through Jesus Christ, with which Anselm is here doing his indifferent best to grapple. I shall do this in five stages. I shall speak first of the redemptive activity exercised by Jesus in the days of His flesh towards the men and women He knew in the flesh; then of the continued effectiveness of this activity as enshrined in the memory of the Christian community; third, of the lesson which this memory holds for us as regards our own redemptive duty towards those around us; fourth, of the new thought of God as Redeeming Love to which it leads; and finally of our crowning Christian conviction that the advent and the life and the death of Jesus were themselves the supreme manifestation of God's redemptive activity towards the human race. It will be understood that all this may be done in a very summary manner, because most of the material of it is already in our minds as a result of the discussions of the earlier chapters.

(i) Regarded from our human end, the foundation of the whole tradition of Christianity as a religion of redemption lies (as we need hardly again remind ourselves) in the love of the Man of Nazareth for the lost sheep of His native land. If I were not afraid that the statement might be overheard by some terribly literal-minded person, I should venture to say that the Christian religion was invented by Jesus to explain and to justify His much-sniffed-at habit of keeping company with publicans and sinners. The Pharisees thought that there were only two attitudes to take to sinners —condemnation and condonation. It was the great discovery of Jesus that there was another —redemption.

How then did Jesus succeed in redeeming them? How did He win men back to goodness? No reader of the Synoptic Gospels can hesitate long about the answer. He won them through the sheer power of His own pure love to awaken an answering love in their hearts. Now in the love which Jesus thus brought to bear on sin we can distinguish two aspects. *First* it appears as a love which, by the power of its own superior loveliness, swallows up wrongs already committed. What mere justice does is to set itself *against* a wrong that has been committed, in opposition and condemnation; and that, on its level, is a great thing to do and, needless to say, infinitely better than doing nothing about it at all. But it leaves us still in the old deadlock of "rights and wrongs." The discovery so richly embodied in the life and teaching of Jesus is that there is a higher kind of goodness than justice, and that this higher kind of goodness does not merely set itself over against wrongs that have been committed against it but swallows them up into itself. This higher kind of goodness is love, and this first exercise of love is what we mean by *forgiveness*. It is undoubtedly this better way of facing evil that is the most remarkable and original feature of our Lord's conduct of His life—how it was His practice to "resist not evil" but to forgive it "until seventy times seven" and "when He was reviled" to "revile not again." Yet no attentive observer could suppose that this forgiveness is mere condonation. It does not amount merely to saying lightly about the wrong which has been done "It does not matter" or "Let by-gones be by-gones." It amounts not to less but to more than that; it amounts to *making* by-gones be by-gones and even, in some true sense, to *making* the wrong not matter.[1] The man who has done his fellow a wrong and has been met not with

[1] "True forgiveness demands positive manifestation of a love which will triumph over the evil past and silence its voice" (J. Oman, *op. cit.*, p. 209).

angry requital but with forgiving love feels that his evil deed has been drowned in the loveliness of this response. Not only does he know that his fellow is no longer thinking of his deed, but he even finds that he himself is not thinking of it, nor indeed of *himself* at all, but only of the love wherewith he has been met and of the wonderful new relationship which this love has called into being.[1] It is this ability which love has, not merely to stand opposed to evil, but in a real sense to destroy it, that makes it the strongest thing in the world.[2]

[1] This does not mean that he will thereby cease to be anxious to make good any overt injury done, so far as that is possible. Nor does it mean that he will thereby cease to feel guilt *towards God* whom, in wronging His friend, he has also wronged: with this further guilt we shall deal under our fourth head.

[2] "The persistent refusal to criticise or to retaliate can be a sign of more life, rather than less, *only when it is a response to a greater degree of truth*. It must mean that the self which has defects or which does injury is seen to be other than the real self; and the non-resistance constitutes an appeal from the apparent self to the real self, or from the actual self to the self that may be. In this case, it is not injustice, but it is justice to the living and the changeable. It is a type of justice undiscovered by the Greek, for it is based neither on equity nor on proportionality to any self that exists. Greek justice, distributive or retributive, took men statically, as they presented themselves. This type of justice refuses to take a man at his own estimate of himself; it insists on the self of a more nearly absolute estimate, the self that *must be*, and which this resolve of the non-resisting will will help to bring into being. It is a justice done for the first time to the plasticity and responsiveness of human nature toward our own wills: it is an absolute, or creative, justice. . . . The creative attitude is not meant to displace but to subordinate the critical attitude, and its varieties, the competitive, the punitive, the warlike attitudes. Antagonism is not an intrinsic evil; it is an evil only when it is not included within a fundamental agreement" (W. E. Hocking, *Human Nature and Its Remaking*, pp. 350 f., 353).

But the love of Jesus was not satisfied when it had cast the mantle of its forgetfulness over the sins of a man's past; it was not satisfied until it had met the problem of the man's future too. And so we come to the *second* exercise to which the love of Jesus was always put—the exercise of *redemption*. When our Lord found a man in the bonds of sin, the deepest feeling aroused in His soul was, quite apparently, not anger, not blame, not a desire to punish, not a scandalized shrinking, not a comfortable sense of His own moral superiority, but an ache to redeem. He must, by the countervailing power of His love, break the hold which sin has over the man's will. He must get the man back for goodness and for God. But now it is to be noticed that this second exercise of love is not independent of the former. For it is precisely the miracle of forgiveness that has in it the power to redeem. It is the turning of the other cheek that wins the sinner's heart. It is the transference of his attention from his own sin to the love wherewith it has been met that lifts him from his despair and gives him heart to make a new beginning. It is the triumph over the past that makes possible a better future. It is his absorption in the loveliness of love that kills the power of sin in his soul.

There is a passage in the Preface to Mr. Bernard Shaw's *Major Barbara* at which I have often stared wonderingly. "You will never," he writes, "get a high morality from people who conceive that their misdeeds are revocable and pardonable."[1] To think that any man could face the realities of human experience and the facts of human history, and say that! I should like to set against it, first a good sentence from one of the late Bernard Bosanquet's early essays, "The truth is that nothing gives such force in getting rid of evil as this belief that the good is the only reality";[2] and then a better one from another source, "To whom little is forgiven, the same loveth little."

But what now, it may be asked, of the particular redemptive efficacy that has been ascribed to our Lord's death on the cross? The answer is, surely, that we have here to do, not with any new kind of efficacy, but with the culminating embodiment of the very same efficacy of which we have been speaking. "It is a mistake," says the Sadhu Sundar Singh, "to think of the suffering of Christ as being confined to the Crucifixion. Christ was thirty-three years upon the Cross."[3] So the final passion of Christ exercised a redeeming influence on the lives of the men about Him just because it was the supreme expression of His love. There has never been a

---

[1]*Op. cit.*, p. 171.

[2]*Essays and Addresses* (1889), p. 124. But, as Bosanquet warns us, "This has been twisted, like everything, as if religion could mean that you were to be indifferent to sin. . . . This is sham religion" (*ibid.*).

[3]See Streeter and Appasamy, *The Message of Sadhu Sundar Singh* (Amer. ed.), p. 132.

better statement of the power of the cross than in the words attributed to Christ by the Fourth Gospel, "And I, if I be lifted up from the earth, will draw all men unto me."[1] And we may remember how once George Tyrrell wrote, "Again and again I have been tempted to give up the struggle, but always the figure of that strange man hanging on his cross sends me back to my work again." In the story of the cross the forgiving and redeeming aspects of Christ's love are blended into a single perfect deed. Christ's death would long ago have been forgotten by the world, if He had died unforgiving, if the saying "Father, forgive them, for they know not what they do"[2] had not summed up the spirit in which He faced His slayers—just as St. Stephen's death would have been forgotten if he had not prayed "Lay not this sin to their charge."[3] And again, Christ's death would long ago have been forgotten, if He had not come by it in the course of His redemptive enterprise, if it had not been a direct result of His ardour in seeking lost sheep—just as Socrates' death would have been forgotten, if he had not come by it in refusing to turn aside from his divinely-appointed mission to the young men of Athens. The wonder of love's willingness to forgive and of love's passion to redeem are, as we have said, what give love its power to save; but when this willingness remains unshaken and this passion

[1] *John* xii, 32.   [2] *Luke* xxiii, 34.   [3] *Acts* vii, 60.

unabated even in face of the ultimate sacrifice, then love's power is raised to its most godlike height.

Surely then our religion is right in holding that vicarious suffering is the most irresistible force that anywhere exists in the spiritual world for the destruction of evil. Surely there is no other power that can do so much to turn us from our sins as another's readiness to suffer pain, humiliation, deprivation and death itself in the effort to win us back to goodness. And I wonder whether it is not in what has sometimes been called 'vicarious penitence' that this power reaches its rare topmost height—when we see another sorrowing for *our* sins, bowed down and broken with grief over the hold that evil has on *us*, weeping penitential tears to God in *our* name. I wonder whether any other element in the sorrows of Christ has been quite so effective unto redemption as this one. Many of us, no doubt, have had some small-scale experience of it in the upbringing of our own families. When a child has done some really evil thing, and when it is imperative that he should be brought to such a sense of the ugliness of his misdeed as will be sufficient not only to prevent its repetition but to wean his heart away from the impulse that led to it, there is nothing that is so likely to achieve this end as that he should see the whole family, who in his eyes are themselves innocent, mourn for the thing that *he* has done. Yet there is ready

to my hand a better example still. In *The Christ
of the Indian Road* there is a chapter entitled
"Jesus Comes through Irregular Channels—
Mahatma Gandhi's Part," in which, among other
things, it is related how Gandhi, when on his release from prison he found his India divided
against itself, Hindu against Mussulman, and
Mussulman against Hindu, first pled and remon-
strated, but finding that of no avail, then "out
of sheer sorrow of heart he announced that
he would undergo, as a penance, a fast of twen-
ty-one days." That was vicarious penitence for
sin, and its immediate effect upon the heart of
India is well described by the writer, who con-
cludes his description thus:

"On the eighteenth day of the fast, Mr. C. F. Andrews, who was editing Gandhi's paper, *Young India*,
while he was fasting, wrote an editorial in which he
described Gandhi lying upon his couch on the upper
verandah in Delhi, weak and emaciated. He pictured
the fort which could be seen in the distance, reminding them of the struggle for the possession of the kingdom; below the fort Englishmen could be seen going
out to their golf; nearer at hand the crowds of his
own people surged through the bazaar intent on buy-
ing and selling. While Andrews watched him there,
that verse of Scripture rushed to his mind: 'Is it nothing to you, ye that pass by? Is there any sorrow like
unto my sorrow?' He ended it with this sentence: 'As
I looked upon him there and caught the meaning of
it all, I felt as never before in my own experience the
meaning of the cross.'

Andrews spoke out in these last sentences the very thought of the heart of India. India has seen the meaning of the cross in one of her sons."[1]

I believe that it is indeed the meaning of the cross and of St. Paul's saying about it that He who Himself knew no sin "was made a curse for our sakes."[2]

(ii) Let us pass now to our second point. It is a very simple one and, after the foundation we have laid, may be dealt with almost in a word. For surely there is no difficulty in understanding how the redemptive efficacy of the suffering love of Christ should be carried over into later history through the medium of His community's memory, and how in that direct and natural way

". . . faith has still its Olivet,
And love its Galilee."

We who in these latter days enjoy the privileges of the Christian *koinōnia* can say, in the same simple sense in which it could have been said by Peter and John, by Matthew and Zacchæus, and by the two Marys, that His sufferings were endured 'for our sakes'; because, if He had not suffered, there would be no Chris-

[1] *Op. cit.*, pp. 100–101. More familiar examples of vicarious penitence might have been taken from Jeremiah and other Hebrew prophets.

[2] *Gal.* iii, 13.

tian *koinōnia* whose privileges we could enjoy. In just this same simple sense the followers of Gandhi will feel in after years that his sufferings were for their sakes, and even in their stead; though indeed one cannot say this without adding, in the words of Mr. Stanley Jones himself, that if during his fast "the silent pressure of the spirit of Gandhi was doing its work in India," yet at the same time "Gandhi's spirit was being pressed upon by the spirit of Christ."[1] It was Christ who taught Gandhi what redemptive suffering meant.

(iii) And so we are led directly to our third point—the significance of Christ's redemptive activity towards those around Him as spurring us on to a like redemptive activity towards those around ourselves. At least half the meaning of the parable of the Lost Sheep is that *you and I* must seek out lost sheep. At least half the meaning of the parable of the Two Debtors is that *you and I* must call out greater love by showing greater forgiveness. At least half the meaning of the cross is that *you and I* should not grudge our very life's blood in the service of our fellows. We were never more true to the spirit of the Man of Nazareth than when, without ceasing to put the sign of His cross on our altars, we began to put it also on our ambulance-wagons; and to paint it on little buildings in our slums where men of brilliant natural endow-

[1] *Op. cit.*, p. 100.

ment were giving up their lives in the effort to redeem their bruised and fallen brothers, or on little huts in the African jungle where a like work of redemption was being done for men of other race. Surely Christ would have recognized all such work as being of one piece with His own and even, as St. Paul says, "as filling up that which is lacking in the sufferings of Christ for the sake of His body, the Community."[1] "To preach the gospel to the poor, to preach deliverance to the captives, and recovering of sight to the blind, to set at liberty them that are bruised" —in reading these words from Isaiah in the synagogue at Nazareth Jesus was laying down the programme, not alone for His own future ministry, but for all true Christian service. And, when it came to the last, He did not bear His cross without reminding those who gathered about Him that they could not become His disciples by merely leaning on His cross and showing no willingness to bear their own. Too often the temptation of Christians has been, in the poignant words of a recent writer, to leave it all "to one great priestly act, one baptism, one cup of woe, though at the heart of all our worship are the words, 'Drink ye all of it.' "[2]

Surely we would have puzzled men less by our preaching about 'the work of Christ,' if we had been more careful to remember its essen-

[1] *Gal.* i, 24.
[2] John Dow, *Jesus and the Human Conflict* (1928), p. 286.

tial oneness with the work which He inspired men like St. Paul and St. Francis, Canon Barnett and Albert Schweitzer, to do in His name.

And even its oneness with lesser works than these. I recently read a true story of how a clergyman in Brooklyn was called to visit a girl who was dying in a cellar. She had for many years cared for a family of younger brothers and sisters after the death of her mother and in spite of the handicaps caused by the habitual drunkenness of her father, and was now at last worn out. The dying girl told the clergyman that she had heard somebody speak of a man called Jesus who would take her after death to the place whither her mother had already gone with Him. "But how," she asked plaintively, "will Jesus know me?" As she put the question, the clergyman's eyes happened to fall on the hands which she had raised in an accompanying gesture, and he was pained to notice how worn and bruised they had become in the service of her brothers and sisters. "Show Him your hands," he said, "and He'll know you."[1]

(iv) After all, however, it is not until we understand why the cross is on our altars that we realise the profoundest element in its meaning. And so we come to our fourth insight—the light thrown by the redemptive passion of Jesus upon the nature of God. It was the teaching of Jesus

[1] The clergyman is Dr. Richard Storrs. I had the story from a printed sermon by Dr. Justin Wroe Nixon of Rochester, N. Y.

that God in His dealings with us eternally is that Redemptive Love which He Himself tried to shew forth in His dealings with the few men around Him during the few years of His ministry. And it is this, certainly, which is the deepest meaning of the doctrine of atonement—not the love of Christ for the people of Galilee in the brief days of His sojourning with them, nor the love that we ought to have for our brothers to-day, but the love which our Heavenly Father eternally has for us who are His sons. I said above that, regarded from our human end, and in the order of our human discovery of it, the foundation of the whole tradition of Christianity as a religion of redemption lies in the love of the Man of Nazareth for the lost sheep of His native land. I say now that, regarded from the end of the spiritual reality which it is our human business to discover, the foundation is rather the love of Almighty God.

It will be remembered that in considering the nature of the love which Jesus was in the habit of bringing to bear upon the sins of those around Him, we found it necessary to distinguish two aspects or exercises of it. First it appeared as a love which cast its mantle of forgiveness over the sins of a man's past, and it appeared, second, as a love which strove to break sin's hold on the man's will and so to secure his future for a higher way of life. There was the love which returned good for evil, and there was the love which sought out the lost sheep. And then we realised that it was the first of these exercises of love that provided the second with the secret of its triumph. It was the goodness returned for their evil that won the lost sheep. It was the miracle of forgiveness that had in it the virtue to redeem. It was love's power of drowning his past that gave the sinner heart for the future. Here we found the secret of our Lord's life; and then we saw how it is also the secret which He has given us for the conduct of our own lives; but now we see that it is far more than either—that it is the secret of the structure of the spiritual universe, the secret of the nature of God.

Let us suppose the case of a young man who has grown up from babyhood in the very best kind of home, surrounded by the noblest examples of unselfish family affection, of transparent honesty, of purity of deed and motive, of the chivalrous treatment of women, of loyal public spirit and of the fear of God. Let us suppose that he himself has first been a charming child and then a fine, upstanding, open-faced boy, not unworthy of the stock from which he came. Then, in his young manhood, other influences come into his life, influences less high and pure, which do something to impair the strength of his purpose and the integrity of his ideals, until at last, coming face to face with circumstances of the most testing kind, he abrogates his manhood by doing a mean and shameful deed. What the deed is we need not specify—perhaps he betrays a friend, perhaps he dishonours a woman, perhaps he cheats another for his own gain or harms another by a lie told to save his own skin, or perhaps he is disloyal to his country. And then, as will so often happen in such a case, he comes to himself.

What now are the young man's prospects? Can he ever hold his head up again among decent people, or in his own home? Has he anything to look forward to but a life-time of remorse, or self-hatred and self-distrust—self-hatred because he has sullied his record and the record of his family, and self-distrust because, having once done a beastly thing, he lacks assurance that he will not do a beastly thing again? Is there any way of escape for him from a future such as this?

There is only one way, and that is to realise that that eternal Goodness which through its human embodiment in his own family circle he had long learned to regard as the one thing worth seeking, and which he has now vilely betrayed, is not a Goodness which merely stands opposed to evil as "an equal and opposite reaction," but is rather a Goodness whose highest virtue is to triumph over evil and so destroy it. Of this quality of the highest goodness he has himself had direct experience in the lesser relationships of his early life; he has himself been prompted oftentimes to meet injury done to him, not with requital, but with affectionate forgiveness; and as often he has been, not the forgiver, but the forgiven. And, if his early training has been a Christian one, then he has found the principle of this forgiveness carried, through the remembrance of Christ's own precept and practice in the matter, to a height not elsewhere known. Thus he knows what is meant by not being overcome of evil, but overcoming evil with good. Now, however, the relation to be mended is not merely between himself and his brother, or between himself and his friend, but between himself and his conscience, between himself and his ideals, between himself and that absolute or eternal Goodness (that αὐτὸ τὸ ἀγαθόν as Plato called it) which has all his life been beckoning to him and striving to win him for its own. And now his one salvation is by faith to rise to the realisation that all our little human goodnesses do at best but feebly reflect the power of this eternal Goodness to blot out the sins that are done in its despite. Here again, if his upbringing has been Christian, such a view of the eternal Goodness lies ready to his hand, in its only quite pure and high form, in the teaching of Him who prayed, "Forgive us our debts, as we forgive our debtors."

The real alternative that lies here before our thoughts is whether such acquaintance as we have with the interrelations of good and evil lead us in the end to regard them as merely opposite forces, whose nature it is to wage war everlastingly against one another, or whether we are led rather to regard the Good as the only ultimate reality and evil as something which the Good can, as it were, in the end unmake or 'blot out' or 'drown' or 'swallow up' or 'absorb into itself'—each may select his own metaphor. The former view finds expression in Zoroastrianism, in Manicheism, and in many another ethical dualism. The latter finds expression in all those philosophies which have followed Plato in identifying reality with goodness. But above all it finds expression in the Christian gospel. For it is only when we see that the highest form of goodness is not justice but *love*, that we see how goodness can have in it the power to blot out the evil that confronts it.

Here alone, then, lies hope for the young man whose case we have been following. He must raise his eyes from his deed to God. He must cease brooding over evil and begin rejoicing in goodness. Ah, he groans, my record has been sullied! But he must rise to the knowledge that what matters is not his record, but God. Ah, he groans again, the evil has been done once for all and stands there eternally! But he must remind himself that only God is eternal and that nothing can stand in the end but God's goodness. He must forget himself and his sin, and remember God and His goodness. To do this is to accept God's forgiveness as in the past he has expected those whom he has forgiven to accept his forgiveness. And in accepting God's forgiveness he also, as it were, forgives himself. To say, "I feel that God has forgiven me, but I cannot forgive myself" would really be to *refuse* God's forgiveness, to allow pride and self-regarding regret for his own damaged record to get between himself and God and so prevent God from doing His perfect work in his soul. Or does he say, "I *must* not forgive myself; it would be *wicked* to forget my sin"? Then the answer is that the only way in which it is *not* wicked to forget our sins is to forget them by remembering God— by allowing the thought of His infinite loveliness to crowd all other thoughts out of our minds, by becoming so absorbed in His service that all self-absorption disappears.[1] "He asks

[1] I cannot understand the view taken by Professor Dinsmore of Yale in his notable and influential volume, *Atonement in Literature and Life* (1906), that "reconciliation is a larger question than forgiveness." "It includes forgiveness," he goes on, "and then stretches out over new experiences and needs. The penitent may know that he is forgiven; but can he forgive himself? Pardon does not perforce make him complacent with his past. His will may have gone wholly over to the good; his heart may rest in a sweet sense of forgiveness; but his conscience may still be a flaming pillar of remorse, and his memory a Gehenna of torment" (pp. 164 f.). "There can be no *reconciliation* without either a *knowledge* of how the dreadful effects of sin are caught up in some providential way and made to subserve a good purpose, or an unquestioning *faith* that in the goodness of God this will be done" (p. 220). "Man and God are not reconciled when forgiveness has been given and received. The consequences of sin must be dealt with, the memory cleansed, the mind made acquiescent with the provi-

too much," said a great saint, "to whom God is not sufficient."

It is this deepest power of divine Love (and therefore, in its measure, of all love) to solve the problem of the sinner's past that is designated by the word atonement. But now the blessed truth is, as we have seen, that it solves the problem of the sinner's future too. The familiar hymn says:

"Be of sin the double cure,
Cleanse me from its guilt and power."

And divine Love *does* work this double cure. The sinner who, by falling into sin, has fallen out of fellowship with God, can never, while thus living in the darkness of remorse and self-distrust, succeed in rising to such a new height of achievement as will of itself atone for his misdeed. He must never try to earn reconciliation with God by mending his damaged record; because, until he has been reconciled to God, he can never have heart or power to mend it.

dential order of the world" (p. 226). Yet what the divine forgiveness can mean, if it includes none of this, I find it impossible to conceive. If forgiveness is not experienced as a sense of reconciliation, then how is it experienced? How could one's heart possibly rest "in a sweet sense of forgiveness" while one's conscience is still "a flaming pillar of remorse"? And to say that, before reconciliation can take place, we must reach the assurance that "the dreadful effects of sin are . . . made to subserve a good purpose" seems to me to ask too much, and more than Christianity ever encourages us to expect—whatever may be true of certain absolutist philosophies.

"Not the labours of my hands
Can fulfil Thy law's demands."

It is the reconciliation that makes the mending possible. It is the loveliness of forgiving love that works the renewal. It is the vision of the Absolute Beauty that breaks sin's empire over the will. Or, in Pauline language, it is the laying hold of the divine rightness that sets wrong men right.[1] Or again, as later and more pedantic Paulinisms would have phrased it, it is the 'act of justification' that makes it possible for the 'work of justification' to begin. Sin, which was once so alluring, now becomes not merely a prohibited thing but actually distasteful; and goodness, which was once so difficult, becomes not merely a thing required of me but actually a thing I love.

"To lie as in an oubliette of God"

—there is no other way than this whereby "the double cure" may be wrought and sin overcome in our souls.

It is this thought of the redemptive relationship in which God stands to our sinning humanity that I believe to be the main burden of our Lord's teaching, from the Beatitudes of His Galilean preaching and His preference of the Publican in the parable to the Pharisee, right down to the words He spoke at the end about

[1] See above, p. 51.

His approaching Crucifixion. It is this thought also, as I have already abundantly argued, that forms the heart of Paulinism. At the centre of everything in the Christian religion stands the fact of God's redeeming love; a love that returns not evil for evil but casts over evil the cloak of its forgiveness; a love poured, not on the righteous and self-reliant, but on weak and helpless sinners; a love given, not as a reward of goodness, but in order to create a goodness which is its own reward; a love that goes out to seek us when we are "yet a great way off"; a love that stoops to conquer, and humbles itself that we may be exalted; a love that goes with us through the valley of the shadow of death in order that we with it may come forth at last into its own larger life.

(v) I pass now to the fifth and final insight which I find contained in the traditional doctrine of atonement and, if I do not dwell on it at length, that is only because what I have said in earlier chapters has already been enough to make it clear that not until we have fully taken it up into our thinking are we able to understand the true power and appeal of the Christian faith. For Christianity has always regarded Christ's discovery of the love of God, not merely as an achievement of human faith, but as an endowment of divine generosity. Nor has it ever regarded the cross as a pattern of God's love which we have been clever to think out for

ourselves, but rather as a pattern of His love
which God Himself devised for our salvation.
The New Testament always looks upon the advent of this Man of Sorrows as itself marking
the culmination of God's redeeming purpose towards His erring human children. In this, it
says again and again, was manifested the love of
God for us, that He *sent* Jesus. Here, if anywhere, I shew you a great mystery, but it is the
very same mystery with which the soul's experience of God is everywhere shot through—
the mystery of a God at once transcendent and
immanent, the mystery of an infinite Personality transfusing our finite personalities, the
mystery of the invasion of our animality by a
higher order of reality, the mystery of the co-
herence of human free-will with divine pre-
venient grace; and, as I have already argued
at length, to find any difficulty of principle in
this part of the New Testament confession is to
deny altogether the active presence in our human history of the cooperating purpose of
God. In His great wisdom God knew that nothing could avail to redeem us from our sinful
ways but the spectacle of One, in whom was the
fulness of His own love, suffering a shameful
death as a direct result of His passion to redeem
us. He knew, in the fine words of Dr. Temple,
that "no man could go on for ever wounding
one who bears the blow like that."[1] And in His

[1] In *Foundations*, ed. Streeter, p. 221.

great love He provided such a redemption. It is thus that the Christ of the Fourth Gospel could say, "And I, if I be lifted up from the earth, will draw all men unto me." It is thus that the impassible God is present for our salvation in the human sufferings of Him who died upon the cross. This is the *mysterium crucis*. This is the Christian salvation. You and me tortured by the shame of past disloyalties, debilitated by the memory of past failures, helplessly unable to pull ourselves upwards by our own dead weight, looking out on the future with a despairing eye; and then the Everlasting Mercy taking the whole matter into His own hands, and making resolve to pour into one chapter of our planetary history, one Man's soul, one life and one death, such fulness of His own loveliness as might have power, by blotting out our past, to make our future securely its own.

I believe, then, that all these five insights— or perhaps, since each is concerned with a "double cure," they may even be reckoned as ten—lie embedded in the traditional doctrine of atonement, and that to omit any one of them from our modern presentation of the Christian message is to run the risk of losing more, in grasp of divine truth as well as in power of appeal, than by our departure from older presentations we have been able to gain.

Does our fivefold or tenfold way of retelling the old, old story seem uncouth and clumsy

when compared with the close-knit and unitary
scheme of an Anselm, an Aquinas, a Calvin?
Perhaps it does. Perhaps the saintly genius of
future generations may succeed in piecing together our separate insights into a tale as simple
and as vivid as the old one, yet without its too
obvious defects. Or perhaps the thought of the
future may not feel the need of this particular
kind of unity. Who can say?

CHAPTER IX

SOME FINAL CLARIFICATIONS

I

WE must now, in a final chapter, do something towards gathering up certain loose threads and ragged ends which have been left on our hands as the result of the foregoing discussions, and towards weaving them into the pattern of the general outlook to which we have found our thoughts leading us. And first we must ask ourselves, Where do these discussions leave us with regard to the doctrine of the Trinity?

It will be remembered from an earlier chapter that we found the Scottish Hegelian theologian, John Caird, making himself responsible for the statement that "the Trinity is the distinctively Christian idea of God." The statement is by no means an uncommon one, yet it is difficult to regard it as other than seriously misleading. What *is* true is that from the third century onwards the distinctively Christian idea of God began to fit itself into a trinitarian mould. But this trinitarian mould, however radically it had in the end to be changed in order to adapt itself to its new filling, was not a thing newly spun by Christianity out of its own peculiar substance, but rather a thing which it found ready to its hand in Hellenistic philosophy. One of the best known and most amusing of the many veiled thrusts which Gibbon allows himself to aim at the Christian religion in his *Decline and Fall* is that contained in the marginal rubric of his chapter on the history of the doctrine of the Trinity: "Taught in the school of Alexandria B. C. 300. . . . Revealed by the Apostle St. John A. D. 97."[1] Gibbon, no doubt, was here working with a very eighteenth-century idea of what is meant by 'revelation,' yet if it were true that the most important and original fact which Christianity has to announce about God is that He is "three-in-one and one-in-three," there would really be something in his taunt.

As a matter of fact, however, the distinctively Christian teaching about God, if it can be compressed into any single phrase, is not that He is triune but that He is redemptive love. True, it has been held by the catholic tradition that His being redemptive love *implies* His being triune, yet it is clear that this implication is by no means peculiar to the Christian idea of God but has, in various ways and degrees, been drawn also from many other and earlier ideas of Him. Indeed we might say that there are few elements in traditional Christianity which it

[1] *Op. cit.*, Ch. XXI.

shares more unmistakably with world-religion as a whole than its tendency to emphasise the number *three* in connection with its worship of the Divine. What has distinguished it from earlier and rival cults is not that it has worshipped Three-in-One but rather the character of the Three-in-One whom it has worshipped. The Hindu triad of Brahma, Shiva and Vishnu and the Egyptian triad of Isis, Osiris and Horus certainly never received the same precise definition (as regards either their threefoldness or the unity underlying their threefoldness) as did the Christian triad of Father, Son and Holy Spirit; yet it is not in this fact, but in the ethical qualities of the triad's members, that the superiority of the Christian 'Way' must be held to reside. And Gibbon was entirely right in believing that the immediate avenue along which this idea of a triad[1] came into the Christian religion was that of Hellenistic philosophy. The fathers of the third and fourth Christian centuries, from Origen to Augustine, were fully conscious of the debt which their thinking here owed to the writings of the later Platonic schools. God, Plotinus had told them, contained in His One Being three *hypostaseis* or 'persons' (as the Latin fathers badly translated that Greek word); the One, the One-in-Many and the One-and-Many; Deity as self-complete, as creative intelligence

---

[1] Τριάς is the term used by the early Greek fathers where the later Latin writers say *trinitas*.

and as immanent in the world. And they could even point to passages in Plato's *Timæus* where the first member of this trinity was spoken of as "Father"[1] and the second as the "only-begotten."[2]

Accordingly, what is most important for us to understand is what those elements were in the characteristically Christian revelation of God which seemed to the theologians of the third and succeeding centuries to flow so easily into this pre-existing triadic mould. When the question is put in these terms, the answer is really very simple. It may truly be said that the members of the primitive Christian fellowship were in the habit of regarding God in three different lights—first, in His transcendent Being as inscrutably above the temporal evolution of the universe; second, as made manifest to them in the love and life and death of Christ; and third, as present in some sort in their own hearts and spirits. And it may be said with equal certainty of truth that these three lights melt in the end into one light—"the light," as St. Paul calls it, "of the knowledge of the glory of *God* in the face of *Christ*" which "hath shined in *our hearts*."[3] That is to say, they looked upon the life of their Christian fellowship as being but a continuation of the life of Christ, and they

[1] *Timæus*, 28.
[2] In the last sentence of the dialogue.
[3] *II Cor*. iv, 6.

looked upon the life of Christ as being but the expression under human and temporal limitations of the life of God. "*Your* life," says St. Paul in another characteristic passage, "is hid with *Christ* in *God*."[1] There you have, in their clear and proper relationship, all three of the terms which were afterwards built into the doctrine of the Trinity. You have them again, stated in distinct triadic form, in the benediction which appears at the end of the *Second Epistle to the Corinthians*, and which has since been hallowed by many centuries of unbroken liturgical use: "The grace of the Lord Jesus Christ, and the love of God, and the communion of the Holy Ghost, be with you all." And once more you have them in the primitive baptismal formula as quoted in the next to last verse of St. Matthew's Gospel (though we cannot look upon it as going back to our Lord Himself): "Baptising them in the name of the Father, and of the Son, and of the Holy Ghost." These two last-quoted passages may indeed at first give to us, who go back to them after centuries of Trinitarian tradition, the impression of having in them some suggestion of the later doctrine that there is a certain threefoldness in the very nature of God Himself, but a closer study of New Testament thought will speedily convince us that this is not the case. As it is put in the *Encyclopædia of Religion and Ethics:*

[1] *Col.* iii, 4.

"At first the Christian faith was not Trinitarian in the strictly ontological reference. It was not so in the apostolic and sub-apostolic ages, as reflected in the New Testament and other early Christian writings. Nor was it so even in the age of the Christian apologists. And even Tertullian, who founded the nomenclature of the orthodox doctrine, knew as little of an ontological Trinity as did the apologists: his is still the economic or relative conception of the Johannine and Pauline theology."[1]

Now what I would say here is this. I do not see that there is anything whatever in the threefold New Testament reference to God the Father, to our Lord Jesus Christ and to the presence of God's Spirit in our hearts, which need give rise in our minds to serious difficulty. As members of the Christian fellowship we must still feel that the spirit of our common life is the spirit of Christ, and again that the spirit of Christ is the Spirit of God. And so we can still, with the very same fulness of conviction as did the early Christians, baptise our children in the name of the Father and of the Son and of the Holy Spirit and pray that our assemblies may be blessed with the grace of our Lord Jesus Christ and the love of God and the communion of the Holy Spirit. But, for all practical and devotional and liturgical purposes, what more do we need? Is anything added, as regards practical effectiveness or liturgical beauty and

[1] *Vide* article on *Trinity* (by Prof. W. Fulton).

continuity, to the simple threefold reference of the New Testament by any mention of "three substances in one essence" or (if the commoner translation be preferred) "three persons in one substance"? I think we shall all agree that for the practice of piety and the proper worship of God we need no more of the doctrine of the Trinity than there is in the New Testament.

This leaves us, of course, with the further question whether, though not for the purposes of faith or practice, yet for the sake of clear thinking we must not follow the theologians of the third and succeeding centuries in finding the notion of "three substances in one essence" to be a necessary intellectual implicate of the simple threefold reference of the New Testament. To this question different answers will be given by different people. Those who are content to regard Christian doctrine as more myth than metaphysic will perhaps claim that we have here to do with the most appropriate symbol which we can ever find for the representation to our finite minds of that Divine Reality whose own self-consciousness must ever remain beyond our comprehension. And so they will say with Canon Streeter that the later dogma of the Trinity, though "arithmetically absurd," is yet "representatively apt."[1] But others will feel differently. They will feel that it is not satisfactory even as representation. And

[1] *Reality*, p. 214.

certainly we do serious injustice to those of our contemporaries who have difficulty with this part of the traditional theology if we speak as if their difficulties were merely intellectual ones (which could therefore be met by the declaration that we are not here on strictly intellectual, but rather on imaginative and poetic ground), instead of being what they certainly are, namely, definitely *religious* difficulties.

The later dogma in question—so let us once again remind ourselves—is that God is to be conceived as being τρεῖς ὑποστάσεις ἐν μιᾷ οὐσίᾳ, which, being literally translated into the Latin etymological equivalents, means 'three substances in one essence.' The difficulty in this formula is that the distinction it emphasises is a distinction without a difference, substance and essence being only two names for the same thing, as was clear enough to the philosophic minds of Plotinus and Origen in that very third century.[1] Accordingly the Latin fathers, beginning with Tertullian, preferred to speak rather of three *personæ* within the one 'essence' or 'substance' (these latter words being now rightly equated with one another); and so in English we have come to speak of God the Father, God the Son and God the Spirit as three different 'persons' united in one essential or substantial Deity. This Latin and English usage, however, so far from making the matter easier,

[1] *Cf.* C. C. J. Webb, *God and Personality*, p. 42.

is just what makes it most difficult to the modern mind. I think the feeling which we have when, starting from a piety that clothes itself in the New Testament language, we pass to the later dogmatic formulation, is that altogether too much seems here to be made of the element of threefoldness that was present in such language. The language seemed natural when we used it and, considering the circumstances out of which it grew, we still believe that it *was* natural; but when we see the use to which the pundits are now putting it, and especially the process of counting to which they subject it, we wonder whether we should not have been a little more careful and a little more explicit. We indeed believe in the Eternal Father whom no man hath ever seen; and we believe that He was in Christ reconciling the world unto Himself; and we believe that His Spirit may be present with us, in our individual hearts and also in our meetings with one another. And we also have something of the feeling that, in thinking of the Divine Being, it is well that we should conceive of Him as thus integrating Himself into the manifold of our experience rather than as a bare and abstract Oneness entirely above the manifold of our experience. But to bind ourselves to the number three, and to find in that a special ontologic significance, is a very different matter. We wonder whether we are after all prepared to distinguish between

God the Father and God the Spirit in this or in any formal way. We wonder again whether we are prepared to say that God's presence in Christ was so wholly different in principle from His presence in other human hearts as this clear-cut distinction between the persons of the Son and the Spirit seems to make it—whether the Incarnation was a fact quite so unrelated to the rest of our experience as this explanation would make it appear. We wonder, once more, whether we do not want to believe that it was the Father Himself who came near to us in Jesus of Nazareth—the Father Himself rather than the second person of a Trinity to which the Father also belonged.[1]

Yet though, for such reasons as these, it may not come naturally to the Christian piety of to-day to express itself by means of the old tri-

[1] Such questionings would have been characterized by our fore-fathers as 'Modalistic' or 'Sabellian' in tendency, but it is obvious that they do not involve us in the difficulties in which such third-century teachers as Noetus, Praxeas and Sabellius found themselves involved. These teachers were all tainted with the two heresies which are most remote from our modern ways of thinking—Docetism and (what afterwards came to be called) Apollinarianism. Their tendency in denying the duality of Father and Son was the totally unmodern one of *identifying* Jesus of Nazareth with God. If we think rather of God, who in some way and degree is present in all our hearts, as being present in Jesus of Nazareth in the fulness of His glory, that through Him He might reconcile the world unto Himself, then the difficulties inherent in Modalism and Sabellianism no longer beset us. And also we can avoid the extreme "Patripassianism" into which the Modalists and Sabellians were inevitably led—while on the other hand being able to escape the equally extreme understanding of the divine impassibility which seemed to be implied in the orthodox formulation, and which rightly gave rise to revolt.

adic mould, let us not make the crude mistake
of casting blame upon the great men of the
third and fourth centuries who gave to that
mould its rigid shape. These men were doing
their very best in the service of the truth they
loved, and it was quite certainly a better best
than any of us would have done if, with the
same equipment, we had been there to see.
What blame there is lies not with them but
with those who sometimes, instead of actively
continuing their efforts, do nothing but lazily
perpetuate their mistakes.

II

Next, let us look briefly at another aspect of
the relation of Christ to God which sometimes
gives rise to difficulty in the mind of to-day.
From the very beginning Christian piety has
thought and spoken of Christ not merely as
One who once lived among us on earth and
now lives away from us in some more blessed
state of being, but as One who can still be present with us, dwelling in our hearts. It is well
known, for instance, how this conception of the
inward Christ—of "Christ in me"—lies right
at the centre of St. Paul's religion. That Christ
should be "formed in us" and should "dwell in
us"—that was what he meant by being a Christian. But now the question suggests itself as to
the relation which this indwelling Christ bears

to the indwelling Spirit of God. Is "Christ in me" simply another name for the immanence of God, or is it the name of another presence in my heart which is distinguishable from the presence of God?

The answer is that neither alternative really does justice to New Testament religion. I think if you had suggested to St. Paul that "Christ in me" is only another name for the immanence of God, he would have replied that he had believed in the immanence of God ever since he could remember, and that even the Stoic teachers of his native Tarsus believed in it, but that, since he came to know Christ, the presence in his heart was somehow different from what it had ever been before, and different, certainly, from anything a Stoic had ever known. But on the other hand I think that if you had suggested to him that in that case there were two presences in his heart—the indwelling God and the indwelling Christ—he would have said that these presences were not two but one. He who indwelt in Paul's heart, and whose indwelling constituted Paul's Christianity, was neither Christ as realised apart from God nor God as known apart from Christ, but only God as manifest in Christ.

In saying this I am not claiming that either St. Paul or any other New Testament writer attained in this matter either to complete consistency of language or to complete clarity of

thought; I am claiming only that their underlying religious feeling in the matter was always
very clear and always very much the same. The
Pauline terminology and ideology are indeed
perplexingly variable. For instance, we read in
Colossians, "Let *the word of Christ* dwell in
you richly,"[1] while in *Ephesians* we read, "That
Christ may dwell in your hearts by faith,"[2] and
in *Romans* we read, "If so be that *the Spirit
of God* dwell in you,"[3] and again, "If *the Spirit
of him that raised up Jesus* from the dead dwell
in you."[4] Now we cannot indeed say that "the
word of Christ," "Christ," and "the Spirit of
God who raised up Jesus from the dead" all
mean the same thing; yet we *can* say that the
indwelling of the word of Christ in our hearts
and the indwelling of Christ Himself in them
and the indwelling in them of God who raised
up Jesus from the dead all mean the same
thing, and point to exactly the same fact of
Christian experience. No reader of the Epistles can fail to feel that in a large number of
cases the Apostle makes an almost random
choice between the alternative terms 'Christ'
and 'the Spirit.' As one scholar has recently reminded us, it would be easy for any student to
fill a quarto sheet with a record of the various
functions which Paul in one place attributes to
the Spirit of God and in another to the inward

---

[1]*Col.* iii, 16.   [2]*Eph.* iii, 17.
[3]*Rom.* viii, 9.   [4]*Rom.* viii, 11.

Christ.[1] And, as Prof. E. F. Scott has well expressed it in the concluding words of a finely-balanced discussion, "The effect of his virtual identification of Christ and the Spirit is to make both of them infinitely more significant. The historical Christ becomes a universal presence, dwelling in the hearts of men; while the Spirit ceases to be a vague supernatural principle, and is one, in the last resort, with the living Christ."[2]

If from St. Paul we turn to the Johannine writings almost exactly the same result appears. The conception of the Holy Paraclete appears here in its most definite form. In the fourteenth chapter of *John* Jesus is represented as promising His disciples that after He has left them the Father will send them "another Helper" (or "Paraclete"), "even the Spirit of truth" who would abide with them for ever; yet immediately afterwards He goes on to say, "I will not leave you comfortless, *I* will come to you"; and in the *First Epistle of John* it is Jesus Himself who is spoken of as the Paraclete whom Christians then had with God.[3] Does this mean that Jesus Christ *is* the Spirit of God? Clearly the writer's answer would be 'No.' But does it mean that the indwelling of Jesus Christ in the heart is the same thing as the indwelling in it

[1] C. H. Dodd, *The Meaning of Paul for To-day*, p. 127 n.
[2] *The Spirit in the New Testament*, p. 186.
[3] *I John* ii, 1.

of the Spirit of that God who was made manifest in Jesus Christ? As clearly, I believe (and
in spite of all confusions of terminology and
overlappings of ideology), the writer's ultimate
answer would be 'Yes.'[1]

Too often in later times the makeshift terminology and ideology of these first Christian
generations were taken more seriously than the
underlying simplicity and directness of their
meaning, and so became the basis either of artificial doctrinal constructions like the later trinitarian formulæ or of equally artificial mystical
'experiences.'[2] But nowadays there are few insights which we treasure more than that of the
real unity and indivisibleness of the spiritual
experience with which we are here concerned.
I shall illustrate this by once more making a
catena of quotations from leading contemporary
writers of different schools. Here is the late
Professor Forrest:

"By no analysis is he [the Christian] able to distinguish his communion with the Father from his communion with Christ."[3]

Here is Dean Inge:

"In no part of the New Testament are we encour-

---

[1] *Cf.* E. F. Scott, *op. cit.*, p. 206.

[2] It was this strain in mysticism, more than any other, which
prompted the Ritschlian reaction against it.

[3] *The Christ of History and Experience* (1897), p. 166.

aged to distinguish sharply between the glorified Christ and the Holy Spirit."[1]

Here is Mr. Stanley Jones in *The Christ of the Indian Road:*

"It is an actual fact of experience that when you deepen the Christ-consciousness you deepen the God-consciousness. Jesus does not push out or rival God; the more I know of him the more I know of the Father. I do not argue that, I simply testify."[2]

Here is Principal Oman:

"Faith in Christ has frequently been so conceived as to be both a burdensome addition to faith in the living God and a misleading substitute for it. . . . No scripture writer ever dreamt that faith in Jesus could be a substitute for faith in God, or a further burden to it, or even any addition to it, or anything except the supreme succour of that faith. . . ."[3]

[1] *Outspoken Essays*, Second Series, p. 50.

[2] *Op. cit.*, p. 59.

[3] *Grace and Personality*, 2nd ed., pp. 143, 148. These passages from Oman are quoted in his book, *Faith in God and Its Christian Consummation*, by my brother, D. M. Baillie, who himself goes on to say: "The answer may seem strangely to mingle the ideas of the Living Christ, the Holy Spirit, and the Eternal Father. But indeed, it can hardly be denied that in this great religious book [the Fourth Gospel] (and perhaps in the rest of the New Testament too) these are but different ways of describing the same experience. . . . The fact is that whenever people take those three ideas, so strangely mingled in the Fourth Gospel, and try to separate them into distinct experiences in their Christian lives, it is extraordinarily easy to distort the meaning of them all and make them all unreal" (p. 263). The whole discussion on pp. 252–264 is relevant.

Here is the late Professor Morgan:

"It is simply not possible to distinguish between the operations of the living Christ and God; and no Christian man tries."[1]

Here is Dr. Herbert Gray:

". . . I cannot see that it makes any real difference whether men say that the spirit of God is working in them or whether they leave out the words 'the spirit of' and say simply that God is working in them. And if others, again, instinctively say that Christ is living in them, as St. Paul did, plainly they are not implying that they are having an experience different in kind from the above. They are really saying, 'The God whom we know through Christ, and with whom Christ was and is at one, is living in us.'"[2]

Here then the necessary clarification seems to have been made. Jesus Christ is not another name for God, but the name of a Man in whom God was, and through whom God came to meet us. The Presence which indwells in the Christian's soul is always this God whom through Jesus we found. On the one hand, it is not a God whom we can satisfyingly know in any other way than through Jesus; for nowhere else than in Jesus has He been satisfyingly present in our world. Nor, on the other hand, is it Jesus Himself, regarded in His separate human self-

[1] *The Nature and Right of Religion* (1926), p. 277.
[2] *With Christ as Guide* (1927), p. 128.

hood; but only that in Him which was God in Him. This Presence we may variously speak of as God the Father or as the Holy Spirit or as the Inward and Living Christ, according as Christian feeling and Christian liturgical use may in different instances dictate.

III

But there is a final question that is likely to be lingering in our minds. Are we really able nowadays to make quite the same exclusive claims for the religious significance of the single figure of our Lord as were made for Him in the Christian preaching of the past? Within a few months of the Crucifixion we find St. Peter (if the account in *Acts* is to be trusted) boldly declaring in Jerusalem that "neither is there salvation in any other: for there is none other name under heaven given among men, whereby we must be saved." And it would not be difficult to parallel this declaration by statements from every other New Testament writer and from the literature of every succeeding generation of the Church's life. Has something of this note been forced out of our modern preaching?

Well, there is no doubt at all that in at least one notable respect we who live in this modern time are differently situated towards such a claim from any of our Christian predecessors, and particularly perhaps from our predecessors

of the Middle and Reformation Ages. By far
the most important and far-reaching of the many
momentous changes which have come over our
religious thinking during the last hundred years
is the new attitude which we have adopted
towards those religious cults which do not own
the name of Christ. During at least fifteen of
the nineteen centuries of Christian history it was
the almost universal opinion of Christendom
that there was no least particle of saving faith
to be found anywhere in the world outside the
rigidly defined bounds of the Christian communion. In Islam, in Confucianism, in Hinduism there was indeed admitted to be present
a certain amount of true knowledge concerning
God and the soul; but it was claimed that such
knowledge was reached only by the *lux naturæ*
and contained no particle of faith or of grace
or of revelation or of anything else that could
avail in the smallest degree for the salvation of
the soul. "Thy best prayers are but as blas-
phemy and sin"—so, with the utmost courtesy
of manner, said the crusading Knight of the
Leopard to the Saracen Saladin in Scott's *Talis-
man*. We are all now agreed that this was great
nonsense. We are most cordially prepared to
allow that along some part of the way up which
God has led us to Himself through Jesus
Christ, He has also led other races upwards to
Himself through other names than Christ's;
and we even find no difficulty of principle in

admitting that in these other and more partial revelations there may be here and there some new gleam of light to which the windows of our Christian tradition should be very hospitably open. Moreover that wistful old enquiry as to how Socrates could be allowed into heaven has lost all its meaning for us. If we were writing a new Apocalypse or *Paradiso* today, we should give the wise man of Athens a place very near the Throne. And so it may be felt that in adopting this changed point of view we have lost something of that note of urgency which has always characterised the proclamation of the Christian missionary message.

Yet here, as in so many other places, the real solution of our difficulty lies in going back to the direct and simple thinking of the New Testament itself. When we do thus go back, there are two very important discoveries which we are at once likely to make, and it is with the mention of these discoveries that I would bring these chapters to a close. The first is that the New Testament claim that "neither is there salvation in any other" is not in its essence an *a priori* theological dogma, such as it too readily became in later centuries, but rather a declaration of personal experience. It is true that when speaking to purely Jewish audiences the apostles showed themselves ready enough to make appeal to the supposedly predictive element in Jewish prophecy in order to prove the divine right of the Christian faith, but nothing could be clearer than that their *essential* appeal was always rather to the results of that faith as actually experienced in their own case. The New Testament writers were not academic philosophers but hard-working missionaries. The problem before them was not the intellectual one of the relative proportions of truth that there were in Judaism, in Stoicism, in Emperor-worship, in Mithraism, in the Orphic rites and in the Eleusinian mysteries, as compared with Christianity: it was the practical problem whether any of these 'ways' could really loose a man from his sins and bring him lasting joy and peace of heart. And their common declaration is that, whatever philosophic minds may say about degrees of truth and the like, yet in *their* experience not one of the many religious alternatives that were at that time before the Mediterranean world could in practice be relied upon (if we may allow ourselves this phrase) for 'doing the trick,' save only the faith of Jesus Christ. What St. Paul wrote to the Greek city of Corinth was not, "There is nothing worth knowing in your local religion or in Stoic philosophy or in Orphic mysticism." What he wrote was, "I determined not to know anything among you save Jesus Christ and him crucified."[1] It was not a theorem, you see, but a plan of campaign. It was not a dogma, but a chal-

[1] *I Cor.* ii, 2.

lenge. And is it not a challenge we can still
make unashamedly, and a plan which, as good
strategists of the Kingdom of God, we shall
still be wise to follow? "I asked an earnest
Hindu one day," writes Mr. Stanley Jones,
"what he thought of Christ. He thoughtfully
answered, 'There is no one else who is seriously bidding for the heart of the world except
Jesus Christ. There is no one else on the
field.' "[1] Now, quite frankly, who else is there?

At the same time there is abundant evidence
that the men of the early centuries were by no
means blind to the fact that there was a real,
though sadly limited, measure of truth and of
saving efficacy in the other religions that were
then known to the Roman Empire—particularly, of course, in Judaism (which from the beginning was put in a class by itself as having
been a necessary preparation for the Christian
revelation), but also in Platonism and in Stoicism. And our second discovery is as to the way
in which they dealt with the problem that was
thus created for their minds. What they did was
to say that wherever in the world there had ever
been any real knowledge of, and effective communion with, the Divine Father, it must have
been because there was there manifesting itself,
in however limited a way and measure, the very
same Spirit and Presence of God as was at last
made fully manifest in Jesus of Nazareth. I say
here the 'Spirit' and 'Presence' of God. These

[1] *Op. cit.*, p. 62.

are the words which nowadays we should most naturally use in such a context, and they were used also in the apostolic age. But in that age, as we had occasion to notice in the earlier part of this chapter, there were certain other terms available which came even more naturally to men's minds. One such term was the 'Logos' or 'Word' of God; another was the 'Christ' or 'Anointed' of God. And, as we saw, these various terms, though having very different backgrounds of meaning and suggestion, yet came at last to be applied in so equivalent a way that often the choice of one of them for a particular context seems to have been made quite at random. The Christian life was said, without distinction, to be a life in the Spirit, a life in Christ, and a life in the 'Logos'; the indwelling Presence in the Christian soul was said, indifferently, to be the Spirit of Christ or the Word of Christ; and that which had been made manifest in the flesh of the Carpenter of Nazareth was said, by different writers and in different contexts, yet with substantially the same meaning, to be God's Spirit, His Christ or His Word. And so, when a Jew would come forward and point to the real revelation of God that had been made in Old Testament history, those early Christians would say, "Ah, that is nothing else but Christ in the Old Testament!"—choosing here the Jewish word 'Christ,' because it was to Jews they were speaking. And when a Greek would come forward and make similar mention of Socrates and

Plato and Zeno, the Christians would say, "Ah, that was the same 'Logos,' who was perfectly manifest in the Carpenter of Nazareth making Himself imperfectly manifest in these others before the time was ripe!"—choosing here by preference the Greek word 'Logos,' because they were speaking to Greeks. So it was claimed that in a large sense even Moses and David and Jeremiah, nay, even Socrates and Plato and Zeno, though living long before Jesus, were nevertheless to be reckoned as Christians, because something of that same Presence of God that was in Him had manifested itself also through them. After the intolerant exclusivism of much later history,[1] it is often surprising, and it is also refreshing, to find how large-minded were the earliest Church Fathers in this regard. "Those who lived in company with the Logos," wrote Justin Martyr in his second-century *Apology*, "were Christians, even if they were accounted atheists. And such among the Greeks were Socrates and Heraclitus."[2]

Now when we read of Christ being in the Old

[1] "Still another merit of the Logos christology has to be mentioned. In the hands of the Apologists it provided a means of relating the culminating revelation of God in Christ with that in nature and in man. It was the same Logos which in its fulness became flesh in Christ that was immanent in nature as its spiritual basis and the principle of its order, and that inspired the Hebrew prophets, the Greek sages, and, indeed, all who had lived rationally and rightly. One must, however, add that after the third century this fruitful line of thought all but disappeared" (Wm. Morgan, *The Nature and Right of Religion*, pp. 190 f.).

[2] *Apol.* I, 46.

Testament, or of Socrates being a Christian and living in company with the Word of God, we are apt at first to regard this as a very odd way of speaking and to suspect the writer of putting a strained interpretation upon ancient history. And it is true enough that the early Fathers were fond of finding predictive references to Jesus where no prediction really was. Nevertheless the main part of our difficulty at this point results from the fact that the word 'Christ' (and to a less extent even the term 'Word of God') has become for us a mere proper name for the Man of Nazareth, equivalent in every way to the name 'Jesus' by which His mother and brothers called Him. And of course it would be more than odd, it would indeed be quite without meaning, to say that we can find the Man Jesus in the Old Testament or that Socrates and Heraclitus companied with Him. But that no ancient Father ever did say, or could possibly be led to say. What they said was rather that the eternal, 'preexistent' Spirit or Word or Christ of God—or, at a later time, the second *hypostasis* of the eternal divine Trinity,—who was made fully manifest in the flesh of the Nazarene Carpenter, was the same Spirit or Word or Christ who had been present in some lesser sense or mode or measure in the experience of Moses or of Socrates, and who had indeed been in *some* sense present since the very creation, and *at* the creation of the world. "The Word of God," as we quoted from

the *Epistle to Diognetus* in an earlier chapter,
"was from the beginning; it appeared anew yet
was proved to be old; and it is always being born
afresh in the hearts of holy men." And it is particularly worth noting, as helping us to appre-
ciate the breadth of the New Testament outlook,
that it is not really Jesus the Carpenter of whom
the Johannine author so often speaks as the
'*only*-begotten Son' of God, but rather the eternal Word of God who was before the worlds
were but who in Jesus the Carpenter alone has
been made fully manifest to our human eyes.[1]
But now, when this explanation has been made,
are we not able to feel that this earliest solution
of the problem of the relation of other faiths to
the faith of Christ was entirely right in principle? Surely it is true that in the Old Testament
and in Socrates, and in Gautama Buddha and
Confucius too, we can find *something* of the
same Spirit and Presence as was in our Lord
Jesus Christ. Surely we ought to look upon our
Christianity, not as excluding, but rather as in-
cluding, the light that there is in other streams
of religious tradition. Surely the only properly
inclusive definition of Christianity is that it is

[1] "Catholic doctrine," writes the late Dean Rashdall, "does not,
it must be remembered, make the human Jesus pre-exist. . . . It
was the divine Logos that pre-existed, not the human Jesus"
(*The Idea of Atonement in Christian Theology*, p. 444). "Clearly
it is the Logos—the Divine Humanity—that pre-exists," similarly
writes Dr. Temple, "The finite centre of consciousness (Jesus)
had a beginning" (in *Foundations*, p. 249 n.).

the religion of all those who love God with heart and soul and strength and mind, and their neighbours as themselves. That, at all events, was the only definition of it that was ever offered by our Lord Himself.

There is indeed one important respect in which our spiritual horizon has immensely widened since these early days. The first Christians worked out their doctrine of the incarnation of the Word of God within a framework of pre-Copernican cosmology which made this tiny planet of ours the one and only centre of God's universe. It had never even remotely occurred to them that there could be other worlds inhabited by spiritual beings just as important as ourselves. We still do not *know* that there are such other inhabited worlds, but we are at least bound to leave fullest room in our minds for the probability. So we find one of our modern poetesses saying:

> "But in the eternities,
>   Doubtless we shall compare together, hear
>   A million alien Gospels, in what guise
>   He trod the Pleiades, the Lyre, the Bear.
>
> O, be prepared, my soul!
>   To read the inconceivable, to scan
>   The million forms of God the stars unroll
>   When, in our turn, we show to them a Man."[1]

[1] Alice Meynell, "Christ in the Universe."

And another we find saying:

"For God has other Words for other worlds,
But for this world the Word of God is Christ."[1]

Yet surely we can apply to these wider reaches
of the divine self-impartation the same principle that the early Christians applied to such narrower reaches of it as were alone within their
powers of conception. Surely we must believe
that the Spirit or Word of God as it manifests
itself in Mars or in some other solar system or

"Far in that faint sidereal interval
Between the Lyre and Swan"[2]

is essentially the same Spirit or Word whose
glory we beheld in Him who dwelt among ourselves, full of grace and truth. If God is truly
One, then His Word must, as Plato and St.
John believed, be "only-begotten" and eternally
the same. And so, in that same sense in which
our Fathers spoke of Christ being in the Old
Testament and of Socrates companying with the
Logos, we of to-day must think of the most dis-
tant fields of inhabited space as not lying beyond
the redemptive reach of that selfsame love of
God which was in Jesus Christ our Lord.

[1]Harriet Hamilton King in her long poem, *The Disciples*;
quoted by Dr. Temple in the essay referred to above.
[2]J. W. Mackail, "On the Death of Arnold Toynbee."

INDEX

INDEX

Victor, Pope, 137.
Vishnu, 187.
Voltaire, 36.

Webb, C. C. J., 192 n.
Weiss, Johannes, 52 n., 63 n.
Westminster *Confession of Faith*, 7, 9, 10, 11.
Westminster *Shorter Catechism*, 8.

Whitehead, A. N., 67 f.
Whittier, J. G., 97, 169.
Wordsworth, 2.

Young Men's Christian Association, 3.

Zeno of Citium, 13, 208.
Zoroastrianism, 177.
Zwinglians, 144.